Her Lavender Valise

Heidi C. Thomas

ISBN: 978-0-578-73701-0

SOME NAMES AND IDENTIFYING DETAILS
HAVE BEEN CHANGED TO PROTECT THE
PRIVACY OF THE INDIVIDUALS.

Her Lavender Valise

PREFACE

To my students-who truly know me better than anyone else. If you let it, there is little that's more authentic in life than the daily classroom.

I've never been a rule follower. Like ever. Besides my own personal unbreakable moral code of being a good human being and loving people as hard as possible, anything else that neatly puts me in a box, dictates useless boundaries, or fills up my time with meaningless tasks leaves me gulping for air. This book will be no different. I am not trying to break new ground, reinvent the literary wheel, or emerge as a unique voice among all the other unique voices. My writing and publishing process will most likely be nontraditional, as I already feel like rebelling against the genre word count rule of thumb that's floating around on the internet. This is a book about travel, self-discovery, everyday life, and fear. It's about art, beauty, and language. In a culture filled with instagrammed moments captioned "living my best life" and "authentic," I longed to read about the day to day creative process of executing your dreams. The regular life grind. The greys of life's essence. I wanted to not only peruse the highlights of being abroad, I wanted to lose myself in the lifeblood of travel. I wanted to, in fact, read my own story. And guess what? I don't even know how this story will end-which is how every true journey should start.

Her Lavender Valise

AMETHYST

"…aids you in knowing you are part of a Universal plan." This phrase about the power of the amethyst…a phrase I had copied off of crystals.net and put into my journal with the Eiffel Tower on it, I knew well. Even as a little girl, I had wanted so desperately to believe in and feel a part of whatever is "out there." Around 5 or 6 years of age, I used to go to this particular set of trees on our treeline whose branches hung down enough to make a little secret spot. It had enough leaf cover that I felt hidden, but little peeks of sunlight came through so it wasn't scary. I used to go there and leave messages and presents for the God I had created in my little girl mind. As far as I can think back, I have been afraid of dying, afraid of leaving my mom's side, afraid of things not being exactly as they were. Around this age, I had overheard my mom on the phone talking to her friend about a mutual friend who had just died from a blood clot in her leg. I didn't understand exactly what was being said; all I knew is that my little body wanted to RUN away. I was consumed with thoughts of dying. I was so shy and attached to my mom and scared of the unknown, that in first grade my mom had to pack me a pickle in my lunch EVERY DAY so I couldn't smell the disgusting cafeteria lunchroom, that did NOT remind me of home. When I was really feeling scared, I would go to this little space in the trees. Sometimes I would write God a note and bury it, asking for answers to all of my questions.

Sometimes I would leave a handful of wilted forget-me-not flowers that I picked in that space, then run and hide somewhere nearby to see if my God would come and get my present. I would go there and cry and rage at my God because no one ever came to pick up the flowers. No one ever found the buried note. In my little girl physical world, I saw nothing to believe. I would constantly fluctuate between being heartbroken that no one was out there and rallying to try again. As I got older, I never lost that. I STILL desperately try to connect to the universe, whether it be through a book, a psychic, or some other kind of metaphysical or spiritual endeavor, like crystals, chakras, or oracle cards. I dabble in it all…and simultaneously provide myself with the same hope and disappointment that 5-year-old me felt.

During one of my many psychic readings in my twenties, I was told that purple was a positive color for me, and I should always wear an amethyst or have an amethyst stone nearby. After purchasing some amethyst jewelry, I looked up the meaning of this gorgeous stone. And there it was…I DID need this stone!!! I DID need help feeling my place in the universe! Maybe this was what I was missing as a little girl, in my secret tree spot? Why my God never showed up to take my handful of limp wildflowers I left? I read this crystals.net definition so many times. I read it when I was feeling inspired and connected. I read it when I was feeling at odds with the universe. Recently, I read it over and over again, as I held the amethyst heart that I had gotten at Elemental Magick, a metaphysical shop in

Sewickley, Pennsylvania. I had gone there with my best friend in the whole world, Andrew, to find something to ground me.

In October of the school year 2018-2019, I had abruptly decided that I was going to take a sabbatical during the Spring of the following school year, 2020. I had been feeling overwhelmed, depleted, and frustrated with life. Even though financially not a great idea for my family, the benefit of taking a sabbatical and focusing on all things French and art seemed the perfect anecdote to my aching soul, as well as providing me some MUCH needed inspiration and a cultural reboot after teaching for 20 years. It was a win-win. After researching French and art history travel programs for Spring 2020, I filled out the paperwork and submitted my application to my school administration. The road to approval proved to be arduous. Not surprisingly, my school had many hoops to jump through. IN MY OPINION, most people who took an educational sabbatical chose to attend a local university and take credits in special ed, STEM, becoming a principal, or reading specialist, and that was what was comfortable for my administration and FIT THE PAPERWORK easily. What I was proposing, to take classes in OTHER COUNTRIES to better myself as a French teacher and bring more authentic culture to my classroom seemed to cause much distress. How would the credits transfer over? What do you mean they don't use the American college credit system? How does one know if these are accredited language programs? How does one even change over the language from French to English on the website to find the answers to these questions? THE UNDERLYING MESSAGE THAT I HEARD WAS WHY COULDN'T I JUST SIT IN A FRENCH CLASS AT SLIPPERY ROCK UNIVERSITY IN GOOD OLD PENNSYLVANIA TO BETTER MY FRENCH???

I understood that what I was asking for was unconventional, but instead of my district being excited for me and proud of me to want to be an overall better classroom teacher and asset to the district, I felt misunderstood and unsupported. Being a foreign language teacher in the United States, especially where I live in southwestern Pennsylvania, definitely doesn't have the same clout as teaching English or Science or coaching football. I jumped through the hoops, provided the justification for each and every part of my sabbatical, helped the admin work through the foreign websites, and finally, I was approved.

However, a few days later, I got an e-mail asking me who would be handling the annual iconic Québec trip that Andrew (also my teaching partner) and I take every year with our students. I wrote back that I would still be going on the trip, that Andrew would handle all the organizing at school, and I had planned my sabbatical trips around my Québec trip. When my administration responded and told me that legally I could NOT participate in the trip if I was on sabbatical, I was heartbroken. Things were NOT working out as I had so carefully planned. I had three choices: 1. To not take my sabbatical at all. After all of my planning and new excitement over my upcoming travel and classes, to NOT take my sabbatical flooded me with a feeling of desperation so strong I went numb. 2. To go on my sabbatical as planned and NOT attend the Québec trip with Andrew and my students. This, too, made me feel sick to my stomach. Andrew and I had worked so hard over the last 10 years on creating a trip that was unique for our middle schoolers. The whole vibe of the trip, the interaction with our students, the first exposures to a foreign culture, the growth that takes place in our 8th graders, were a direct manifestation of our teamwork. There was NO WAY I could just hand this off to someone else. 3. Change my sabbatical to the Fall of 2019. Given my choices, the only thing I could do was change my sabbatical. I was angry because I had PLANNED for the Spring of 2020. I had no money saved for my trips or my classes that I was funding one hundred percent on my own. I had to abruptly come to grips with NOT starting the school year with my students and leaving them with a sub. I had to get my classroom cleaned and organized to have someone else in there for a semester. I had to contact all of the courses to reschedule for the fall. IT WAS NOT WHAT I HAD PLANNED.

But...who would have known that life for the WHOLE WORLD in the spring of 2020 would come to a screeching halt??? I could never in a million years have dreamed up the world events that snowballed in the beginning of 2020. After participating in my sabbatical classes in the fall of 2019, I returned to the classroom in January of 2020, and COVID-19 hit shortly after. Teachers were ripped from their classrooms, country borders closed, and the world was basically quarantined. It was…and is…a most unprecedented time in travel. It took me a couple of weeks into quarantine to realize the enormity of the pandemic. If I would have followed through with my initial plan of a sabbatical during 2020, it actually would have never happened. All of my travel abroad would have been cancelled. CANCELLED.

Since I abruptly had to leave my classroom to someone else for a semester, I spent the last few weeks of school rigorously spring cleaning my room, which included taking every single thing out of every single cabinet (a teacher's nightmare!!!) and going through it. Because of this, when COVID hit, my room was easy to pack up during this bizarre event. Another gift. And it was my truest great fortune that my district was able to find a most incredible French substitute, who loved my students as much as I do. She is now a treasured friend of mine. GIFT.

Through a lot of freaking out at the universe, all of my swearing, all of my selfish, bratty screaming into thin air to my "guardian angels" about WHAT I NEEDED TO DO TO GET THINGS TO WORK OUT FOR ME WHEN I SAID, the universe was there all along. Quietly supporting me and working things out. MY universal plan. I still am unable to fully FEEL how unbelievably lucky I was. The gratitude that I experience when thinking of all of this is so much bigger than my emotional capabilities. To say that it stops my heart, halts my breath, freezes time, gives me goosebumps is completely inadequate for the magnitude of the gift I was given. One of many lessons I learned throughout this time. I am still in the infant stages of being able to let go and trust the bigger plan that I am a part of, but the foundation has been laid through *Her Lavender Valise.*

THE WHITE...AND THE BLACK

"You are a free spirit trapped in the conventions of a traditional life," the psychic said, sitting cross-legged across from me in her home in the spiritual community of Lily Dale, New York. She continued, "You'll never be rid of that, because you love both worlds. The key, my dear, is to honor the free spirit part of you more. Don't hide her away. In doing so, your wild child tends to break out every ten or so years and goes NUTS." The psychic eyed me. "You know what I'm talking about."

My mom, my sister, my cousin Rachel, my late grandma, and my late Aunt Lin have always been interested in ghosts and spiritual activity. As a child, I remember begging my grandmother to tell me stories about how her house was haunted. How there was a ghost of a woman named Edna who lived in her attic. When my sister and I played at her house as little girls, we always stood at the attic stairs and looked up, whispering about what the lady in all white looked like. As a college student, I took a class called Folklore and Legends. For our final exam, we had to interview someone who had experienced paranormal activity and was passing those stories down through the generations.

I interviewed my grandmother, on a tape recorder, (it was the early 90's) and transcribed our interview for the Clarion University archives. She talked about seances and loud, manly footsteps that echoed through her house that didn't belong to anyone. She told me how there was a room in her house where they had let a doctor quietly perform abortions for women who had nowhere else to turn. That same room, years later, was where my mom, as a teenager, and her friends had a séance that supposedly summoned the dead that haunted that space. About 20 years ago, we had our first psychic party at my house. And by we, I mean my mom, my sister, my cousin Rachel, and my Aunt Lin (who passed away last year). This intensified my interest and belief in the spiritual unknown.

At some point along the way, we discovered Lily Dale, New York. Every summer, usually in late July or the beginning of August, we would make the 3 ½ hour drive up north to Lily Dale. There, we would spend the day walking through the quaint, peaceful streets of this unique, gated community that was full of psychics and mediums. We would attend the daily stump reading, which was a group reading in the middle of a forest clearing, where a lineup of psychics would give random readings. We always packed a huge picnic lunch, which we ate under the picnic shelter. We would talk and share our paranormal experiences while we ate. After lunch, if anyone had enough money saved, we would go our separate ways to have private readings with a psychic. This is where I found myself that afternoon, in a small sunroom connected to my psychic's house, full of crystals and windchimes and garden gnomes hidden among the blossoming hydrangeas.

My mind, and my pulse, immediately started racing,

as the psychic's words sank in. THE TRUTH, I thought.

The whites of my life are colored inside the lines of tradition. I grew up with two amazing, supportive, Catholic parents, who are still married and are my neighbors. I went to college, got married, and am raising two perfect, blessed daughters. I live on an old family farm, my grandfather's dream, where my parents have four acres, my sister and her kids have six acres, and my husband, two kids, and I have six acres. We all share a driveway, have family dinners, get each other's mail, and run necessities to each other's houses in an emergency, like toilet paper or olive oil. On a nice evening, we all meet at various points on the driveway and walk. I'm a teacher and coach, and I have worked tirelessly to truly love every student and athlete I've ever been in contact with. I shop at Whole Foods and in the organic section of Giant Eagle. I am grinding HARD at this traditional thing. Like just now, my dad drove my garbage cans up from the bottom of our shared driveway and stopped in to tell me about the black bear that was spotted down the road. I am comfortable with this me…other people are comfortable with this me.

My free spirit side that the psychic had brought up thrives on the intense, the beautiful, unharnessed emotion, freedom, connection, and pure love, my blacks. I definitely do NOT respond well to being told what to do. Oh wait…you want me to sit through a bunch of worthless meetings and fill out a lesson plan just because??? No thank you. My Spotify is a constant revolving surprise of Chopin,

Cardi B, Rage Against the Machine, Dixie Chicks, Mozart…you get the picture. You want me to go out with a large group of people for happy hour and listen to inane, mind-numbing small talk? While I do adore a good buzz (and an ice-cold Tito's with club soda and lime), I'd rather be at home than subject myself to that boredom. I could never, ever be in a relationship where my partner told me what to do, or where I had to "ask" to do or have something. My free spirit is a hard core, tough as nails, emotionally charged bad ass, who comes at things and people at full force. I've learned throughout my 49 years to shove that part of me down, a lot, in order to make others comfortable. Be smaller. Be less. This, however, as I thought about what the psychic had said, has not proven to be effective in honoring myself.

Every fifteen years or so, I become so suffocated, so BORED, so overwhelmed with WHAT does any of this mean???? that I literally lose it.

There was that time during college, when I was so bored with the emptiness of academia and the "faux" intellectual conversations that were carried on around me in coffee shops in a haze of smoke and combat boots, that I turned to partying really hard and many boyfriends just so I could feel SOMETHING.

Or the time, years later, when I had two young baby girls, was a stay-at-home mom, my husband's first business was going through a bankruptcy, and I felt so much fear and oppression of what typical "adulting" was that I spent nights sitting in my car after everyone had gone to sleep, drowning myself in trip hop, Yellowtail Shirazz, cheese Pringles, and Marlboro lights.

Fast forward to now. I feel on the brink of another break. The meetings, political bullshit, and busy work at school have far surpassed the purpose of being an actual teacher. School has become a business. Standardized testing, state ratings, the UNENDING empty meetings, the daily grind, the working so hard just to get by. Every year, the state and school districts around the country add more and more to our already full plate as educators, without taking anything away. These meaningless, but time consuming, tasks drain so much of my energy that little is left of me to devote to growing myself as a teacher. My classroom environment, as well as my teaching style, are based on the relationships created with my students. Those relationships drive my curriculum and continually fuel my passion. I have had a constant mental and emotional battle the past few years as I struggled to get everything done AND create new exciting material. Can you say BURNED OUT??

My impulsiveness and rebellion find a way out again, but this time I chose to be a little more productive than Pringles and wine. Without much planning, thought, or emotional dwelling, I decided on this sabbatical for the first semester of the school year. Not only would I be engaging in a series of professional learning opportunities that included travel, art, and the French language, I decided to take these next 5-6 months to truly get to know myself, face some old fears, and uncork that place that I keep closed where my desires and dreams reside. I spend so much of my days living in my neatly drawn white lines that my blacks, my passions, have been left to smolder. And I am doing this all solo, for the first time in my life.

First stop?? Florence, Italy. For a weeklong course in the Italian Renaissance and its impact on Europe. A city where I had visited for a few short days the previous year and immediately felt like I had found a missing piece of myself. A city that can only breathe in a state of ecstasy…in colors of garnet and deep ruby red…colors that permeate your being and stain your soul. I just know this is the city that can transform my sleeping embers into a powerful onyx gem. Inside this deep black magic of the onyx is the stillness of night, where fears are freed and awakenings follow.

JUST THE BLACK

"You are the most comfortable uncomfortable person I know." Bill said, looking across the high barstool table at me in the Breakneck Café.

I don't think anyone in the world has a best friend like I do. Bill has been my best friend for 34 years, ever since he sat behind me in 9th grade English. I hadn't really known him previously at school, as we were in two different types of friend groups. However, every time I turned to pass back a paper to him in our row in class, his mischievous smile and smart ass comments would never fail to make me laugh out loud. He is super smart, wickedly sarcastic, extremely observant and intuitive for a guy, and the best listener EVER. We were inseparable. We would literally spend HOURS driving around in his little Toyota Tercel, smoking cigarettes, listening to Metallica, Pink Floyd, or Zeppelin, talking about everything or not talking at all. He was there to hold my hair back when I would throw up after drinking too much, when we first started experimenting in high school. He was there to listen to every boy drama I had…and to come to my rescue when I made bad decisions. When I left for college and he stayed at home that first year to work, I counted the minutes to when my dorm phone would have a double ring (signaling an off-campus call), and I would settle in on the floor under my peach wall phone to talk for HOURS. When I went away to Québec for the summer for my

French immersion program, he and our other best friend drove 36 hours there and back to my college to see me, just for the weekend. He ended up attending the same university I did, and our friendship continued to deepen as we both worked our way toward adulthood. He watched me get married, and he was there when I had to have my appendix out on my wedding night. I was in his wedding. We each had two children who are the exact same age. When he built his house by himself, I used to come over with a cooler of Yuengling beer and sit and keep him company while he worked. We joined a gym together when we hit our 30's and felt like we needed to get in shape. Nowadays, we live close by each other, but only see one another maybe four times a year, when we go out for a night of drinks and catching up. I look forward to every second of those nights, just as much as I used to look forward to the 9:30 p.m. hour of our high school youth, when he would get off of work at the local hardware store and I would get off work at Phar-Mor, which meant it was time to hang out. Our friendship is like no other for me…it is seasoned with every high, every low, of life…youth, college, marriage, raising kids, divorce, loss, death, reinvention of ourselves, aging. Bill really knows me better than I know myself. He has never judged me (and BELIEVE ME, there has been a lot to judge over the years), I never, ever get bored of him, and there is never, ever enough time for all of our conversations. On this particular night, we were pretty deep into Titos and self-analysis, our specialty.

He continued. "You are, and always have been, attracted to the extraordinary. It is so easy for you to find that little bit of specialness in your students and all you meet and celebrate that. Yet you are uncomfortable with recognizing and falling in love with your OWN extraordinary." I let his words wash over me, thankful that things were a little soft and blurry, as things get with alcohol.

I knew he was right. I had let all the times where I felt small, or felt too much, drown any true connection or love of myself in scarcity. I have TONS of ego driven fear, which have left lots of uncomfortable holes in myself. I am constantly trying to fill up these holes; I always overdo everything past the limit-too much of a certain food, obsessing about a relationship with the WRONG person, celebrating WELL past the celebratory point, too many clothes, shoes, shopping…you name it!!! I like to blame all of that on the pleasure-seeking Taurus in me, but I know deep down it's much more than that. Because of all those little holes, I'm always in a state of feeling emptiness that can never be filled. I yearn for situations that are impossible. Then, I feel emptier because I can't access them. I am the QUEEN of excess in every way. Can anyone relate to this??? Even though I didn't realize it then in college, I see now that I almost loved, in a twisted way, the day after partying too much, when I felt sick, exhausted, and smelled like old cigarettes from the frat house I was at the night before. This gave me something specific to "clean up," a PROCESS, taking away my focus from my feelings. I literally did the same thing every time after a night of indulging: wake up early because I can't sleep; fight incredible nausea; eat Lipton's Noodle Soup; watch vapid romantic comedies; order a pizza; finally take a shower; go to bed early to have a "normal" day the next day.

Same with my house. I never keep up with house cleaning maintenance, THE GRAYS, even though it is so easy to do. It's easy to load the dish washer every night, wipe off the sinks after they are used, put laundry away after it comes out of the dryer, to make a grocery list. But instead, I watch as things slowly disintegrate into a hot mess in my house after a few weeks. And I go to the grocery store every day, with the excuse of being "European" instead of me really just being disorganized. I watch as my house becomes a complete mess, cat fur, dust, showers with soap scum, until I can't take anymore. Then I freak out and spend a whole week meticulously cleaning each room, top to bottom, on my hands and knees, until every crack and crevice is shined to perfection. My house is either a showroom, or not presentable for a visit. It's my PROCESS.

I do this with my body, too. I will do, and complete, any hardcore exercise challenge. I did an 8 week paleo crossfit challenge. I did a 30 day hot yoga challenge. I did the 21 day fix challenge. When they are over, though, I can't seem to incorporate any of the things that I learned or did into my everyday life. It's all or nothing for me.

BLACK OR WHITE. *And in between are all of my PROCESSES for getting from one extreme to the other.*

For some reason I don't understand, I refuse to live in the grays. I FEAR the grays. Interestingly enough, this is the exact thing that fascinates me about French culture. I remember the first time I watched a French film. It seemed to move so slow compared to our American blockbusters. You would see people brushing their teeth, going to the bathroom, getting dressed: THE GRAYS. The everyday things are not only noted, but they are completed with passion: the daily shopping at the markets; the way they value quality over quantity and size in their homes; the lingering over meals. There seems to be no need OR desire to fill with stuff. There is no need to be in the EXTREMES at all times just to feel, because there is a beauty and emotion in ALL of the things, whether it be making your bed or looking at the *Mona Lisa* at the Louvre. The blacks and whites that I am constantly consumed with build up over time. It's like a decanter of wine that's been filled too full…then you put the stopper in and wine flows out over the top and runs down the sides. Some of it stains; some of it gets wiped away; some of it is left on the sides to dry, sticky and hardened, forever changed.

I went for a walk around my property, unable to get what Bill had said out of my mind. Alone with the hushed liveliness of nature, I stopped in my backyard. My backyard. Pure. Untouched by landscaping, chemicals, pruning, edging. Where weeds grow as freely as the wildflowers and grass. At night, sometimes, while searching the clear sky for the Big Dipper or Orion's Belt, I can feel the true vastness of the universe. I've lived and walked these paths my whole life. This was a place where friends would sneak out to, and we would stay up all night smoking cigarettes and dreaming out loud until the sun came out. A place where we fell in love, out of love, and everything in between. A place that holds as many secrets as it has blades of grass. A place where I still live. I was struck today with how something so raw and wild and basic can still hold so much beauty and abundance. New beginnings are like that...raw, rough around the edges, a little scary, but still full of beauty and promise and LIFE. I have so much to look forward to in my next endeavors.

Florence, where the chianti flows as freely as the passion, be my teacher.

Florence, Italy, January 2019

"I saw the angel in the marble and carved until I set her free." -Michelangelo

I love that first glass of wine, when the warmth spreads from the inside out and the edges soften, blur. But somehow that wasn't the case in Florence. From the first bottle of Chianti Classico in a little café in the Piazza Della Signoria to the last bottle of this dry, cherry, peppery magic, every sip just brought this captivating city into sharp focus.

We spent a few days wandering through the Piazzas, breathing in the ancient beauty of the statues and the Cathedral of Santa Maria del Fiore. I bought a gold bracelet from a jeweler on the Ponte Vecchio, the famed stone bridge with brightly colored buildings jutting from it. We took part in a wine tasting dinner at the Verrazzano Winery that looked straight out of the movie Under the Tuscan Sun.

Creamy polenta with tangy sauce topped with spices and crushed red pepper with Chianti Classico. Fresh Marguerita pizza with Chianti Classico. Homemade tagliatelle bolognese with wild boar and Chianti Classico.

I stood in the center of this Roman city, where the intersection of the axis is marked, and felt the energy coursing through me as I imagined the Romans in their original forum. I bit my lip hard so as not to cry while standing in the Medici Riccardi Palace, listening to our guide retell the tragic myth of Orpheus and Eurydice...

Everywhere I looked, turned, breathed, listened was passion, pure beauty. Finally, a place where my heart felt rested and my breath full and open. All my life, I've been told, in one way or another, that I'm too much…too much emotion, feeling, intensity. And here I found myself, standing in a city that literally EXISTED ON TOO MUCH.

And then…there it was… Michelangelo's <u>David</u>. Exquisite. <<God, how can people breathe when this, this art, is your city??>> Our tour guide asked us to simply put our phones and cameras away, and he drew our attention to the sculptures lining the walls on the way to <u>David</u>: Michelangelo's <u>Slaves</u>, or <u>Prisoners</u>, all in various stages of completion. I was entranced by the figures that appeared trapped in the marble, trying to free themselves into complete human form. I felt weak as I identified with Michelangelo's work. As I let my eyes fall on each one, I felt parts of me melting away. All the years that I had enslaved my own self with busyness, just so I didn't have to feel as much. The extra schoolwork I would stay up all night doing. Coaching not one, but three cheer teams at a time, on top of working full time. Giving everyone in my day every piece of me until I had nothing left.

Right there, right in the Accademia Gallery, I let go of imprisoning myself. And with the new space that I created by that release, the deep intensity that I had buried in my own marble began shining through the cracks.

And all of this freed spirit, this reinvigorated adoration for art, along with a bottle of Chianti Classico, I packed in my lavender valise.

"EVERYTHING ABOUT FLORENCE SEEMS TO BE COLORED WITH A MILD VIOLET, LIKE DILUTED WINE." -Henry James

Florence, Italy, September 2019. I want to remember everything exactly as it is…but HOW. Sitting in a café in Piazza della Signoria at 3:30 pm on a Thursday, sipping Prosecco, I thought about tomorrow being my last day as I look at a larger than life fountain of Jupiter. How can this be my normal? When I really think about what's actually happening, my breath catches so hard my heart stops for a moment…

I once sat beside a girl on a flight coming back from Paris, who told me that she felt that each city she had ever visited took on the persona of a male or female. She said that to her, Paris was a tall older gentleman who smoked cigarettes and wore a black fitted coat, reading a newspaper in a café drinking strong coffee; and that Beirut, where she was from, was a young woman who had long flowy hair and wore a light dress and bright smile while dancing barefoot through the city. I loved that. How each city had a personality that you could just FEEL. For me, cities are music, a VIBE. And Florence is a music snob, of course, classical Baroque…Vivaldi, Bach, Handel…full-bodied, rich, refined, gilded.

When I arrived in Florence around 9 am Sunday

morning, I just KEPT MOVING. If I stopped, I would have been frozen in fear. I rolled my lavender valise right out the door of the airport and searched for the taxi queue. A taxi pulled up and a man hopped out, loaded my suitcase and turned toward me with a gentle smile. I showed him the address to my hotel on my Booking App. He made polite broken English chit chat and made me feel at ease with his open laughter at my comparison between drivers in Naples and Florence. And 25 euros later, I was there in front of my hotel. A wave of fear started bubbling up as I longingly looked after my taxi, for some weird reason not wanting him to leave me here alone. My eyes darted around nervously at my street, Via dei Calzaiuoli. OMG I WAS HERE ALONE. TRAVELING ALONE. IN ITALY. My family miles and miles away. I took in one high end boutique after another…Chanel makeup boutique, the famous Benheart leather boutique, Swarovski…Okay. This should be fine. JUST KEEP MOVING. Because I arrived well before check-in time, I had to use the code that had been e-mailed to me through Booking.

The building I was to call home for the week was a mixture of apartments and hotel suites. I was staying in a suite. I carefully read the instructions for getting in the building and made my way to a little reception office. There I met Jasmina, the sweetest woman EVER, who checked me in. As luck would have it, my room was actually ready. I felt so grateful…I was exhausted both emotionally and physically, starving, and really wanted a shower.

I almost cried real tears of happiness when I saw my room. I stood in the middle and took it all in. The gorgeous herringbone floor…the green marble shower…the double windows that were opened up to the courtyard below, where I could hear fellow travelers talking and laughing as they shopped and ate gelato. The delicate cookies that were placed under a glass dome. The room was absolutely spotless. And I had it all to myself. I was overwhelmed.

I took a hot shower and got ready to explore my surroundings. For each of my travel experiences during my sabbatical, I chose a fragrance to wear exclusively for that trip. That way, whenever I was yearning for a little bit of Europe or Québec back at my home in Pennsylvania, I could just put on one of my chosen fragrances, and I would immediately be transported back. For Florence, I chose Mediterraneo by Carthusia. Last summer, I had the opportunity to take a trip of a lifetime with my friends and my sister to Europe, and one of the places we stayed was Capri, Italy. In Capri, we visited the Carthusia boutique, and I fell in immediate love with their Mediterraneo. The lemon and green tea scent evokes the luxurious, lemony Italian island, and I thought it would be a perfect complement to Florence. Jasmina had given me a street map of Florence and highlighted the main areas. The city of Florence was fairly small, definitely walkable, and divided up in to 4 main areas, each one known for a church and a piazza.

You guys…this was my FIRST challenge…to get around by myself. I am literally the WORST when it comes to directions, reading maps, etc. I am definitely a follower when it comes to getting around somewhere. I used to teach at a private school in the city of Pittsburgh. One day, this farm girl here decided to go to Whole Foods during my plan period, which was like five minutes from my school. Somehow I got confused at the street called Penn Circle, made a wrong turn, and ended up in the bus lane AWAY from any streets that cars drive on, AND facing the wrong way. I was hysterical-called 911- and the police came and had to escort me back onto a regular street. OMG. And I had a class of 7th graders waiting for me back at my school. All because I wanted an organic salad from Whole Foods. If that story didn't illustrate my complete lack of any basic understanding of directions, maybe this one will. A few short years ago, my friends and I set off on a whirlwind tour of Cologne, Amsterdam, Rome, and Paris. While in Amsterdam, my friends decided to pay a visit to a local coffeeshop. And this was not for an iced decaf mocha with almond milk. Coffeeshops in Amsterdam are where you smoke marijuana. Legally. My friends all partook in this cultural pastime, while I chose NOT to. We had only been in Amsterdam a few hours, so hardly enough time to figure out the layout of the city. So when it came time to seek out some of Amsterdam's infamous pancakes, out of the four of us, three high out of their minds and me, guess who got the map? Yep…it was me. We spent HOURS walking over the many bridges of the city, past hundreds of bicyclists, with me leading the way with the map. My stoned friends trailed behind me, completely oblivious to the fact that I had literally been leading them in the same square, over and over again, unable to get us to pancakes. Several hours later, we gave up and went to the first restaurant that we came to. My friends all thought it was hilarious that we couldn't find the pancake house. But I was sober? I was not stoned?? The next morning, we started off on our walk to the Anne Frank House. And, just around the next corner, was the pancake house that we just couldn't get to yesterday, because of my map reading skills. My sober map reading skills. That story is a running joke with my friends, that I am sure to never live down. Anyway, that's how bad I am with directions. And yes, I could use Maps on my phone in Florence to help, but I was terrified of having my phone or purse stolen. So a paper map it was.

As it turns out, where I chose to stay couldn't have been a more perfect location. I walked to my left, and suddenly, I was among the Florence Duomo/cathedrals, with their signature white, green, and pink marble façades. First order or business? To find a *farmacia*, a pharmacy, to buy tampons. Nothing like having to figure out day to day life in another country. After awkwardly being stared at by three male pharmacists, I managed to explain what I needed and hurried out the door.

I was shaking from hunger, so I sat down in the

closet café to the farmacia. My first solo meal in another country. I let out my first deep exhale since arriving and looked at the view from my café table. Steps in front of me rose up the dizzying beauty of the Catedral de Santa Maria del Fiore. I dined on a salad of fresh, creamy buffalo mozzarella, ripe red tomatoes, fresh basil, and olive oil drizzle. I ordered a dry white wine and bottled still water to accompany my salad. When my food and wine arrived, I just stared…I couldn't believe I was here. I made it. I DID IT. I was in this dream. I was in Florence.

An older couple from California sat next to me and invited me to share a bottle of Chianti Classico with them. We chatted about traveling and tattoos and dragonflies. I must have started to fade into that second glass of wine, because the gentleman gently nudged me and said, "Don't fall asleep at the table!" We parted ways. Earlier when I had first set out, I had every intention to walk the path to where my art history class was being held the next day, but my exhaustion had gotten the best of me. On my way back, I slowly meandered through the tourists window shopping on my street. I was ready to collapse, but I joined the long line of people waiting to get a taste of gelato from the famous Venchi, rated one of the best gelato shops in Florence. It was just a few doors down from my place. I ordered my favorite, *stracciatella* (chocolate chip), to eat on my way back. It was only about 3:30 pm, but I was DONE. I relaxed in my room, talked to my family, set my alarm for EARLY, and crashed.

The next morning I woke up at 6 am, already kicking myself for not finding my school the day before. My class started at 10 am, so I calmed myself down, knowing that I had time.

I opened my double windows out to the little alley below. Unlike yesterday, all was quiet in the early sunlight. I took a shower, grabbed my street map and class itinerary, and headed out to figure out where exactly I was. I walked past many little bakeries, where people were already standing at counters having espresso. Restaurant and café owners were setting up outdoor tables and umbrellas. Delivery trucks were zooming precariously through the tiny alleys, dropping off cases of Acqua Panna water to businesses. Jasmina, my girl at the check in, told me it was just a ten minute walk to my school. I had already been walking for fifteen minutes. I must have gone too far? Missed a turn somehow? I reluctantly got out my cell phone and turned on Maps. I just needed to backtrack a little. I had been so busy looking at my map and for street names, that I wasn't really noticing what was around me. I was definitely in a piazza, not one of the more famous ones, but nonetheless enchanting. A little more up the street and there was Via Ghibellina, the street where the Accademia del Giglio is located. I cheered quietly to myself, happy that I had found my school.

I glanced at my phone and saw I had plenty of time to grab some breakfast. Diagonal from my school sat a little café, nondescript but friendly looking. I honestly don't even know what the name of it was. But this place quickly became part of my routine before class. Each day I would come here, via Piazza della Signoria, and eat a croissant (*cornetti*) with custard in the middle and drink a *cioccolata con panna* (hot chocolate with whipped cream). For those of you who are lovers of the French croissant, Italian baked goods are NOT the same. The Italian croissant is much denser, heavier, and usually has a sugar coating of some sort on the top. I'm not a baker, but I think it has something to do with the use of butter in the French dough? They are both delicious, but I prefer the light layers of the French croissant.

After eating, I would meet Barbara, my art history instructor, at 10 am for our lesson. Each day we would take on a different museum. The week seemed to melt into one long, sweet day…the museums chased each other in my mind, like the spirited bubbles that wind through golden hued prosecco in a flute. Barbara and I sat on a bench in the Santa Maria Novella Church, in front of one of the original frescos of the Italian Renaissance, discussing our own personal connections to art. We walked the long corridors of the Uffizi Gallery, where I lost my breath so many times as my eyes took in masterpieces of Botticelli and my first favorite artist, Titian. Barbara took me through the Palatine Gallery where the Medici family lived, and we stood and looked into the eyes of all the portraits that were hung and tried to reconstruct their personalities. We walked the Boboli Gardens, where Barbara sat on a bench and let me wander on my own. I walked around fountains, through pebbled walkways lined with lemon trees that dated back to the Medici family, and ran my hands over moss covered sculptures, patinaed with age. In the San Marco museum, I was drawn to the monks' quarters and stood at the doorway of each one, every stark stone room peppered with an original Fra Angelico fresco. In the Medici Chapel, Barbara made me close my eyes, and she grabbed my hand and led me into the Chapel of the Princes. She had me look to the ceiling, which was covered with such magnificent art that I kept a hold of her hand, squeezing it hard, even after I had opened my eyes. My

 favorite, though, was the Bargello Museum. The Bargello was a former prison which now held all the Renaissance sculptures. A moment that is burned into my mind is when I stood face to face with Donatello's *David*. Italian sculpture has such a hold on me…I've always been inexplicably drawn to it. These masterpieces are the epitome of luxury, extravagance, and such loveliness. You want to own my heart? Put me in a wild garden with aged Italian sculptures hidden by some greenery, Mozart playing, a bottle of wine, and I'm yours for life. Not even kidding.

Every inch of Florence was art. My senses were in overdrive, and my heart exploding. I let each museum become a part of my energy. I was slow, deliberate in my studies. I was also slow with my meals. At home, I am on the run CONSTANTLY; you know, the typical American household, where kids are in every single after school activity and sport, you eat in the car, and there isn't enough time in the day, and then you do it all again the next day. Here in Florence, I lingered over EVERY meal. I thought about every bite I was eating, every sip of prosecco. I celebrated my meals: fresh bruschetta, homemade pasta with the sweet tang of stracciatella cheese, and a margherita pizza so delicious, I had it twice. Each meal punctuated by a light honeydew tasting prosecco (if it was lunch time) or a lusty Chianti Classico if it was dinner. During *Aperitivo,* the Italian happy hour, I went to the same café every day, where I had a bitter orangey aperol spritz and munched on Bugle chips (OMG remember those???? I didn't even know they still made those!) and salty green olives. I sat alfresco, eating and drinking, without rushing, without looking at my phone, without stress. To just BE, alone in an outdoor café, taking such care with my meals, watching the world move past, was surprisingly heavenly. These were perfect moments to let all the gorgeousness of the day's studies fill every inch of me. To not have to explain, or justify, or tone down my emotions was liberating.

Florence, you have been a most profound teacher, and I, your most devoted student.

Martha from Arkansas

The second day of my classes in Florence, in the morning, I was assigned to meet a different prof other than Barb at the studio. For a few hours, I was assigned to an actual art instructor who was going to teach me hands-on Fresco techniques. Now, I'm sure most people who study art history, let alone travel to Italy for an art course, are gifted in actually CREATING art. I could not draw a stick person, nor was I interested in learning how. My knowledge of art was me ordering a reproduction of Roy Lichtenstein's *Masterpiece* and juxtaposing it with a charcoal black wall in my bedroom. My knowledge of art was historical, emotional, intellectual...mostly emotional. Art made me feel like I BELONGED...to something...even if that something was created in my mind. Like when I stood in front of the Warhol soup cans, those red and white Campbell's soup can labels immediately connected me to the daily label that was our physical universe. But there were also the clean lines...that as I stared at them I imagined the Velvet Underground's avant-garde boundaries.

It wasn't always this way for me, this affinity I had for art. Like most teenagers, I found museums to be excruciatingly boring. And I especially hated modern art, which is so funny to me because it's one of my favorite art genres now. I remember looking at a Jackson Pollack and thinking WHAT IN THE ACTUAL WORLD IS THIS.

How could all of these random paint splatters mean anything?? Then, my junior year of college, that all changed. I was double majoring in English and French, and I needed another humanities class to fill the 18 credits I had to take every semester that my heavy major required. I chose Art History 101. Sitting there in that class, listening to my professor tell the story behind each painting and tie the style, brush strokes, colors, etc., to the historical time period and any political/cultural movements blew my mind. After that class, I felt like I could look at any piece of art and become part of the story, regardless of whether I liked the style or not.

Anyway, here I was, with a morning of learning how to create an original fresco. At the Accademia, I was led through a hallway off the main check in room where I had paid the balance of my tuition and met Barbara the day before. All through this hallway were people set up at easels in various stages of work, punctuated with big jars of paint brushes, half-finished pieces, Roman sculptures, and green plants. I have never felt so out of place as I did at that moment. I felt like a fraud. I giggled to myself as Courtney Love's lyrics "…I fake it so real, I am beyond fake" popped into my head. Me…with no artistic ability (or desire to actually CREATE art); me…with limited historical knowledge in a city whose spirit was THE CENTER of everything art; me… just a middle school French teacher searching for SOMETHING in her mundane suburban routine. As I walked through all the people working on whatever was on their easels, I felt that everyone could sense my duplicity. My grey linen shorts, leopard sandals, and flowy bohemian silk blouse, while adorable for museum visits, did not seem practical for painting and sculpting, and only enhanced my insecurities now. I was led to the very back room, which held large buckets of limestone, tiles, and sharp hand tools. There was another woman there, working quietly on a sculpture. She was probably in her fifties, was wearing mom jeans and a baggy, stained tee-shirt. Curly brown hair framed her plain, but friendly face. She had a streak of plaster on one of her cheeks. This woman did not seem to notice me as I came into the room, but I could not take my eyes off the contrast of this nondescript woman and the beautiful form she was working on. This was Martha, from Arkansas.

She worked quietly while my instructor asked me in broken English what level my artistic ability was. She seemed to not notice as I explained that I had ZERO ability...none, which left my instructor flabbergasted as to how to even begin with me for my fresco lesson. When he left the room to get supplies, Martha finally looked up from her work and smiled.

"Based on your accent, you must be from America." She smiled. "Hi, I'm Martha, from Arkansas."

Happy to have a friendly diversion from the stress I was feeling over my fresco lesson, I introduced myself to Martha. She went back to working on her sculpture as she talked, continually wetting her hands and molding the plaster beneath her hands. I learned that Martha's dad had passed away in the beginning of this year, and she had suffered a great bout of depression. Feeling like she had to do something different with her life, she set out to experience Europe and to take art classes in Italy. She said, "Honey, where I'm from, people never leave. It's the same people, the same small-town life. There's really nowhere anyone wants to go, you know? I had only left one time before, to travel to a different city in my state, to attend a workshop on sculpture."

Not only had Martha never been out of the county before, she had never been on a plane before. And to top that off, she decided that since this was a trip of a lifetime, that she was going to see as much of Europe as she could. SOLO. She had already been to London and Paris, and after Florence, she was heading to Amsterdam. She had limited funds, so she stayed on the outskirts of every city she visited. She told me she took the bus into the heart of Florence where the Accademia was, but walked the five miles back to her place at the end of each day because she couldn't figure out how to read the bus schedule. She had a little bag with a plastic container in it that held her lunch. My cheeks burned a little as I thought about how I was staying in the luxury heart of Florence, really like a seven minute walk from my hotel, and I had been scared out of my mind to search for my school on the first day. Here was this woman, with no travel background, no cultural background, no foreign language background, spending six weeks in Europe away from her husband and dog, alone, following her passion. I was IN AWE. All my fears and worries seemed nonexistent in comparison.

Hearing Martha's story, I was instantly brought back to my very first trip to Europe. It was 2013. Here I was, a French teacher since 1994, and I still hadn't been to Europe. With all of my panic and anxieties that have plagued me since I was little, the idea of getting on a plane for more than two hours sent my claustrophobia into overdrive. The idea of leaving my home, my daughters, my family, THIS COUNTRY, was really just unbelievable to me. I did NOT grow up thinking that traveling was a possibility. What if I had a panic attack while I was gone? What if something happened to my young daughters while I was gone? What if I got sick? What if, what if, what if????? I eventually decided to go that summer of 2013 with my three best friends. Actually, "best friends" does not do our little group of four justice.

There's Andrew, whom I have already mentioned, who teaches French with me. There's Greg, who taught German in our department. And finally, there's Amy, who is the Latin teacher. Our group friendship is the most beautiful, unique, wild, interesting ride I've ever been on. Our connection defies description. It's a glorious mix of intelligence, open-mindedness, unbounded fun, and respect. If I was ever going to get my ass over to Europe, it would be with these three. I knew they would make me feel safe, acknowledge my fears without making me feel stupid, and be patient with my eccentricities the whole way through. I was fragile, and they knew it, without me having to say it.

That first trip was a whirlwind of three countries and every major landmark; one morning we were touring the Vatican in Rome, and that evening we were taking an elevator up the Eiffel Tower. My friends kept my anxiety at bay for the most part. But that first trip, I refused to drink a drop alcohol. I was PETRIFIED that I would have a panic attack, and what could be done so far away from home? I remember when we had arrived in Rome, we checked into our apartment and went to explore our piazza, which just so happened to be where the Pantheon was located, Piazza della Rotonda. We were in this adorable café, right across from the Pantheon, and I just couldn't relax enough to even recognize the unbelievable beauty of that moment. I remember our waiter asking me what wine I would like to drink, and I said, "no wine for me, grazie." The waiter exclaimed, "But *Bella*, you are in Italy, no?!" I held my backpack tight to me while I ate my tomato and buffalo mozzarella salad, sipping my still water.

I ventured over to Europe again in 2017. My friend Andrew was going to be married in Italy, and, of course, we were all going. I was in a panic, because I wanted to be celebratory for the wedding, but how did I know how I would react to European alcohol? Still couldn't risk it. For that trip, I purchased about 30 little airline size bottles of Titos. I bought bubble wrap from the post office, and I wrapped each one of those little bottles up and put them in a make-up case. My girlfriends who were going to the wedding and I decided to go to the South of France for a few days before heading to the wedding. That first night, overly tired from two long days of travel, I gave in and had a cold glass of white wine in a Thai restaurant in Nice. After experiencing no panicky side effects, I slowly started experimenting with French wine. It has not failed me yet. Oh my, how far I've come since that night sipping water in the Piazza della Rotonda.

Looking at Martha's little plastic disposable container of a packed lunch, I became acutely aware of my own privilege. Here I was, seeking out the best cafés in Florence for the best lunch experience. I HAD to stay in a hotel that was centrally located among all the luxury that Florence had to offer, so I could feel safe. I am in a constant state of internal conflict where I live in Pennsylvania. I live, and teach, in a fairly affluent suburb outside of Pittsburgh. It's full of new money, a lot of entitlement, and every single possible advantage to kids. I have lived here my whole life, before this area became the exclusive place that it now is. So I'm a bit grounded in old school ways, but I also adore the luxuries and privileges that living and working in this kind of area give. My own kids have had every single thing they could ever imagine, except living in a housing plan with a paved driveway (and granite kitchen countertops). I despise the narrow, pampered view of my area, but I love rolling out in the morning five minutes down the road to Starbucks to pick up my tall, iced, decaf, 4 pump mocha, almond milk, no whip coffee that I get every day. Hypocritical? Conflicted?

Not sure which one I am.

I was painfully, and exuberantly, feeling my gratitude, and embarrassment, while Martha talked. Painfully aware of every extra construction job that my husband worked so I could stay somewhere nice in Florence. Aware that our bills would not necessarily get paid on time. Aware of the sacrifice. Aware of the hard work. Aware of cashing in part of my 401K that I JUST STARTED last year to pay for my sabbatical. Aware that our bank account went down to ZERO every single month.

Simultaneously, I knew that my struggles, although real to me, were not really of any consequence in the world view. There were many who would long to have the struggles that I do; you know, taking a semester off to travel to Europe and such. I am constantly aware of the word CONTEXT. Daily. And what that means for each of us.

It was at that moment, I decided to throw away all of my insecurities of not being an artist. I was here to embrace life…to embrace this Italian experience, in every single way, not just the ways that I was comfortable with. I rolled up my silk blouse sleeves, put on my Parisian readers, and dove in. My instructor came back and walked me through how to actually create a true Italian fresco, like how they did it from the beginning of its inception. In a bucket, I mixed powdered lime with water, with my hands, to form a sandy paste. When that was ready, I put the paste on top of a ceramic tile, and formed about ½ inch thickness with my hands, smoothing and sculpting until the tile was covered evenly. While that dried a little, my instructor suggested that I pick from a bin of old photos and painting replicas, since I couldn't draw anything of my own. I chose a Degas that had three ballerinas. The next step in creating my fresco was to take that Degas, and using an old nail, poke little bitty holes alllllll around each important line on the paper that formed the outlines of the picture. That took a while, poking all of the little holes. Once finished with that, I was given black charcoal and a dry sponge. I put the picture with the holes punched in and set it on top of my drying limestone tile square. Taking the sponge that had been dipped in the black charcoal powder, I rubbed it all over the little holes, pushing the black powder through. The end goal is for the outline to be present on the tile once the paper is removed. Finally, it was time to paint!! I was given a pallet with some pure pigment powders on it. I was instructed to mix the powders with water to paint onto my tile. If I wanted different colors other than what was there, I was to mix what I had together to create an additional pallet. Martha and I talked the whole time I worked. We shared cultural stories, travel fears, and life questions. Painting my Degas was definitely the hardest part of this creation. All the beautiful, light-filled blues, greens, golds, and creams that were so significant to this famous Impressionist's works came across as heavy and somber, almost autumn like. As I was beaming with pride over my subdued ballerinas, my instructor came over, clearly at a loss for words for my elementary work. However, he kindly said, "Not a typical Degas, but I like your color interpretation." Giggling as he left, I began to collect my things to move on to my museum visit for the afternoon with Barbara. I hugged Martha from Arkansas tight. I told her how much I respected and admired her for her endeavors. We were no longer two individuals from different states, with different backgrounds and life experiences; we were two WOMEN, strong, united, fighting fears, living out dreams, and kicking major ass. I am convinced that Martha was an angel that was sent to me from the universe. Throughout the rest of my sabbatical, whenever I felt scared, unsure, uncomfortable, or alone, I would remember my morning with Martha…a morning full of limestone dust, dirty hands, and true female camaraderie.

*****

But not every moment was amazing, though. During my sabbatical, I also wanted to face old, buried fears and release them. One of those was panic. Most of my life, up until after my second daughter was born, I battled severe panic. Panic attacks that would seemingly come out of nowhere and paralyze me. I've driven myself to the hospital more times than I can count, thinking I was dying. When I was in college, which was the height of my panic, I would drive myself routinely over to the Clarion Hospital emergency room. There, every time, the doctors would check my heart, sometimes do an EKG, sometimes give me oxygen. There was never anything wrong. I've had to leave my classroom as a new teacher. I always sit on the end of a row in a movie theater or auditorium in case I need to leave. I've slept in a chair sitting up because of panic. Oh my, the debilitating moments are scary even writing about them. My flight game is STRONG. Whenever I would be having a panic attack, my response would be to RUN…somewhere…anywhere. I would try to outrun the panic, to leave it behind in the dust. It would always start off the same way. Something, whether it be caffeine (which I no longer drink), alcohol, lack of sleep, stress, would cause my heart to beat fast. Once I noticed the feeling of my heart beating fast, I would freak out BECAUSE it was beating fast, which would cause it to beat faster. I would become lightheaded because of the panic, sure I would faint (but I never did). I was PETRIFIED.

Then, in order to match my fast heartbeat, I would run or pace or walk quickly, trying to escape the feeling. This could last for hours. This anxiety was a HUGE part of why I never traveled anywhere far throughout my life. The idea of an anxiety attack happening while I was across the ocean was enough to put me in a state of pure terror. As I've learned what triggers my panic attacks over the years, they have become less frequent, almost nonexistent…but not quite.

So here it was, Thursday in Florence, almost the end of my first solo travel experience. I was feeling particularly celebratory. I was celebrating myself, for accomplishing this huge milestone, for attending an art history course, for navigating the streets of Florence alone, for flying across the ocean alone. All of it. And I was excited to be heading home soon as well. I DID IT. Tomorrow I would have my last class, and then I'd need to pack, as I had an early morning flight scheduled to Barcelona to meet my friends Michael and Trenton for a few days before returning home together.

Feeling light, fun, and a bit feisty, I started my celebration at my favorite café in the Piazza della Signoria, Caffé Perseo. I ordered bruschetta with bright, fresh tomatoes and a half bottle of Prosecco. Feeling giggly from my Prosecco, I went back to my hotel room to drop off my bag that I carried during my class. While in my hotel room, I decided to further my celebration by indulging in another half bottle of Prosecco from my minibar. Then, of course, things unraveled into a blurry mess of me facetiming my friends at home who were just getting off work and drinking the bottle of wine in my mini fridge. By this time, I was definitely drunk, and, remembering my daughters' warnings of not going out while I didn't have all of my faculties about me, I had to make do with what was left in my mini fridge for a late dinner. I finished off two small cans of Pringles, a mini bag of almonds, and the cookies that were left under the lovely glass cake dish every day after my room was cleaned. Tired from all of the celebrating, I drifted off to sleep.

I awakened sometime in the middle of the night, probably around 3 am, to a bunch of text messages and missed calls. The missed messages were from my friends Michael and Trenton, whom I was meeting in Barcelona. Apparently, there was in airstrike in Spain, and most of the flights that weekend had been cancelled. My head cloudy and full of rocks from drinking, I reached for the nearest bottle of water, recoiling when I realized I had taken a swig of sparkling water, when my palate was thinking still water. (I'll never get used to that in Europe…having to request STILL water over sparkling). I drank my carbonated water, and I read the e-mail that had been sent to me from Easy Jet, the airline I was taking from Florence to Barcelona, indeed confirming that my flight was cancelled. Panic hit me, and hard. The alcohol, lack of sleep, and now fear of how to navigate the travel world in a foreign country by myself overwhelmed me. AND OH MY GOD I COULDN'T RUN ANYWHERE. I was trapped, in Italy, in my hotel room, ALONE, in the middle of the night, with a panic attack. My worst fear coming true. Heart racing, breath shallow, sweating, I had NO CHOICE except for to sit with my panic. There was no running from it this time. After throwing open my double windows and gulping the fresh air with my head hanging out, my mind raced. I should have never thought I was strong enough to travel alone. I was so far from home. I looked on my phone at my LIFE360 app. Just the image of seeing my face in Europe and my family all in Pennsylvania was enough to push me over the edge. I threw my phone into the covers on my bed. I guess I'll just die in here. No one knows I'm having a panic attack. There is no one here to help me. I am utterly alone. Feeling like a trapped female tiger at the zoo striding back and forth in front of the bars, I began to pace.

As I paced back in forth in my room, my mind flashed back to a couple of years ago. I take my French students to Québec City every year. They are 8th graders, and for most of them, my trip with them is their first trip away from home, not to mention to a non-English speaking place. And I don't just take 20 of them. I usually have 75-100 students that go with me, my French teaching partner and best friend Andrew, whom I previously mentioned, and a few other core chaperone/friends. This particular year, I had a girl student who suffered from major anxiety, in addition to some other ailments. One of the nights we were there, she called me from her hotel room to tell me she wasn't feeling good. We had already done room checks, and all of the other chaperones were tucked into their rooms as well. There was something in her voice that told me that she was having an anxiety attack, which was why she wasn't feeling good. Without even thinking too much about it, I knew what I needed to do. I grabbed one of the other chaperones, and together we went and got her from her room. I told her we were just going to walk together, no big deal. I saw, for the first time, myself during a panic attack in her. I saw the fear in her eyes. I saw the need to escape. TO DO SOMETHING. To make it stop. Because we were in a hotel, I knew we couldn't outrun the panic, which is what I would normally do. Instead, we walked. We walked for hours. Up and down hotel steps. Around the lobby. Up to the very top floor then down again. We walked THROUGH the panic. There was no way out...only through. And while we walked, I talked. I talked about nothingness, then I talked about having anxiety myself. I talked until I saw her face soften and become engaged in the conversation. I knew the panic was passing. We kept going, though. After a while, she was an active participant in the conversation. We giggled while we took selfies in front of the empty boutiques in the lobby because it was the middle of the night. The panic had passed. My student went to bed smiling...tired...and empowered.

My mind kept racing faster than I could process. My heart the same. If I could help someone else through this, I could help myself. So I did with myself just what I did with my student. I walked...slowly...around my hotel room. Because my room was one of two suites in an apartment type building, there was really nowhere for me to go outside my room. I walked slowly in a circle, talking out loud to myself. I talked about my day to myself. I talked about the event with my student in Québec. I talked out loud about all the art I had learned about this week. I walked in circles around my room. I kept this up until my breathing regulated, my heart rate slowed down. I felt like the crispy edge of paper that had been caught on fire with a lighter…like the edges of the love letters I used to burn in middle school. And I knew I was through it. Exhausted, I flopped onto my bed and looked at the time. It was 6 am. The sun was coming up, and it was time for me to get into the shower for my last day of class in Florence. I was on the other side. Me. By myself. Handled a panic attack in Italy. Alone. I felt like something significant had just shifted in me.

You know, in school people always talk about what the students are learning in your classroom. What verb conjugations did they learn that day? How is that vowel cluster pronounced? What's an infinitive? And of course, that's all very important, but I will tell you that my students teach ME every single day. The fact that I was able to deal with my panic attack the way that I did I learned from my student. She taught me bravery, trust, and fortitude. There are other students that gave to me during this trip. My first day of my art class here in Florence, I posted a pic on Instagram of some of the monuments and museums that I visited thus far. Gigi, Camille, Thomas, and Victor R.

(their French names, *bien sûr*) all sent me messages throughout my trip and/or commented on my picture, wishing me good luck in my class, telling me how proud they were of me, how excited they were to share in my travels, and that they missed me. These students will never know how I LIVED for these messages. Those brief comments gave me confidence to take on my class and embrace my experience. They gave me love and connection to help me fight through my loneliness. I am forever grateful for these classroom gifts. And this is just a teeny tiny peek into what my students gave me during my travels. The wealth of what I have learned from the hundreds and hundreds of students I have taught over the past 20 years is pure gold. I probably have learned the most about myself *in the classroom*. You cannot hide yourself away when standing in front of 30 students 8 times per day, day in and day out. They know when you didn't get enough sleep because you are wearing your glasses instead of contacts. They know when you are in a good mood. They know when you spilled your morning mocha on your pants. They know when you change from your winter perfume to your spring scent. They know what you eat for lunch. They know when you are stressed based on the number of Hershey Kisses wrappers in the trash. They know when your throat hurts and when your allergies are bothering you. Students know the real you, whether you want them to or not. My students taught me what unconditional love feels like. This is the authenticity I wrote of in my Preface.

When I got out of the shower, there was a text from my friend Michael. He had found a flight for me to Barcelona and had already booked it and paid for it. Gratitude, pure and strong, flowed throw my body. For the moment, all emergencies were handled.

The other shoe dropped later that morning. Exhausted and emotional from my night of little sleep, I had my last day of class...and said good-bye to my prof Barbara, who had become a friend during this week. I decided to go have lunch at my favorite pizza place across the Ponte Vecchio, Santa Felicita Ristorante. Halfway through my margherita pizza, my phone rang. It was my daughter Genevieve. Although it was lunch time in Florence, at home in Pennsylvania she should have just been getting up for school. "Mama?" Genevieve said in a small voice. "Mama? I think I'm having an allergic reaction, and I'm here by myself. Daddy has already left for work." Genevieve is my youngest daughter. She is a junior in high school. Genevieve has, since she was an infant, many food allergies, including dairy, eggs, and all peanuts and tree nuts. How could this be happening? We are always so careful with food, and she is so well educated on what she can and cannot eat. How could this be happening??? My mind racing, I threw 20 euros on the table and started running back to my hotel room. After making sure that Genevieve could breathe and swallow and she had taken Benadryl, I kept her on the phone as I raced across Florence back to my room. Realizing that she was more frightened than in serious danger, I kept her talking, kept her connected with me, as I waited for the Benadryl to kick in. She went from being scared about a possible reaction to a protein bar that she ate (that she eats every day) to worrying about missing school to crying about missing her football game later that night (she's a varsity cheerleader for her school). I started to detect the drowsiness from the Benadryl. And, even though I was across the ocean, I told her to rest her eyes, to stay home, that I would handle everything. She said softly, "Thank you, Mama. Even when you are in Italy, you take care of me." When we hung up, I called my sister to go over and sit with her while she slept, to make sure her breathing was okay. I called the school to let them know she would be absent. I texted her cheer coach to let her know she would be missing the game. And I stayed in my hotel room the rest of the day, checking in with her every half hour. After the adrenalin rush had faded, I sank down onto my bed, my head in my hands. Jesus. Well, I had naively wanted this solo travel sabbatical to be about personal growth and facing old fears. However, what had sounded romantic in my mind when starting out had become reality, and one that I was NOT prepared for. I had envisioned a kind of Hollywood *Eat, Pray, Love* transformation, where I would find all this self-development in the bottom of a pasta bowl with Michelangelo's ghost as my witness. Not me walking ludicrously in circles around my hotel room, talking to myself, and my daughter having a medical emergency thousands of miles away from me. But therein lies the gift... THE UNIVERSE KNEW I'D HAVE TO BE IN A

SITUATION THAT I WOULD HAVE TO
SURRENDER COMPLETE CONTROL. Although still
a frail, scared child in my mind rather than the strong,
empowered, confident woman I aspired to be, I saw that I
have taken baby steps towards my future self. And I did it,
alone, in Italy.

Oh CAVA, where have you been my whole life?

I didn't return home right away after my class in Florence. I was off to meet my best friends Michael and Trenton for a long weekend in Barcelona. I had never been to Spain before, and I was so excited to study Antoni Gaudí's work. And truly, after my first solo week away, I was really happy to be with people again.

Michael and Trenton have been a part of my life since 2014. We first met through the world of competitive cheerleading when they started coaching my two daughters. A short time later, we ended up coaching two competitive teams together, and from that point on, they became my family. They are both in their 20's, so much younger than me, but for whatever magical reason, we just click together. I stood beside Michael as his Matron of Honor in his marriage to Trenton. We've traveled to New York City and Québec City together. We've spent many an evening laughing and sharing life's ups and downs, and eating a lot of Mad Mex. I've never met two more genuine, beautiful human beings. Although it's only been six years, I feel like I've loved both of them my entire life.

It was a whirlwind of a weekend. We visited Park Güell, Casa Batlló and Casa Milà, and of course the ever famous La Sagrada Familia church. The contrast between the geometric plurality, patterned tiles, and curved architecture inspired by nature in Gaudí's work and the classical antiquity of Florence was absolutely fascinating to me. I found myself engrossed in the mysterious, politically complex, thrilling Catalan culture. It was different for me with Spain than with Italy. When in Italy, I just feel like I'm a part of the Italian soul. In Spain, I felt like I was chasing an aloof, bewildering, smoldering man whom I was both afraid of and attracted to. However, during this chase was when I discovered my love…my obsession…with cava.

I must embarrassingly admit that I knew nothing of the Spanish culture coming to Barcelona, let alone the Catalan culture, which has its own thing going on separate from Spain. I really didn't know about the food, the wine, the customs, etc. The first night, we went to eat at a Michelin star restaurant. When the waiter asked us what we wanted to drink, I said to just bring me some kind of white wine, as I didn't know anything about Spanish wines. OH my friends…here is where the education starts. The sommelier there suggested CAVA, which turns out is Spain's version of prosecco or champagne. From my first sip, I WAS INNNNNNNNN. I have always been a fan of the bubbly. When I was in college at Clarion University in the 90's, I had my Alpha Sigma Tau squeezie bottle filled with the cheapest champagne shit possible while others filled theirs with beer. I was a connoisseur in the making. I've come a long way since drinking bottom shelf champagne out of my sorority water bottle, but cava was a whole new experience for me. For starters, the bubbles were more intense…almost bigger and steadier. The flavor? Not as sweet as prosecco, still fruity, but almost

EARTHY. I was hooked…intrigued. Cava was so…BARCELONA. I tried some other unique Spanish things: tapas, paella, parma ham, bombas (meat and mashed potato ball, fried), but the cava had me won over one hundred percent, searching for more.

One of the activities we scheduled while in Barcelona was a guided bike tour of the city. When I travel to new places, I like to use the WITH LOCALS APP. You can schedule food tours, bike tours, museum tours, really anything you want to get exposed to and learn about a brand-new place. Our guide for our bike tour was named Seth. Seth was originally from Belgium. While biking around Barcelona, Seth taught us about everything we came across, from local customs, to food, to politics and architecture. But the best little tidbit we got from Seth was about cava. Seth told us that there was a little hole in the wall cava bar called Can Paixano, where only locals go. AND they bottle their own cava. He said this was the only cava bar of its kind in Barcelona. Of course, I had to try it.

On our last day in Barcelona, we spent the early morning in Park Güell, in Antoni Gaudí's home. Our plan was to hit up the cava bar before lunch, as it opens at 9 am. We thought that would be a good time that wouldn't be so busy.

We found the super small, standing room only bar a little before noon. It was already packed with locals. The Spanish language, high energy, and wall to wall people spilled out of Can Paixano onto the sidewalk. Michael,

Trenton, and I froze. As much as I wanted to get in there and experience this cultural cava phenomenon for myself, I was scared. None of us really spoke Spanish, and we really looked like outsiders. How in the WORLD were we going to push through all of those locals, with next to nothing language skills, and blend in? I was INCREDIBLY intimidated.

We decided to go across the square and have lunch instead and come up with a game plan. Over pulled pork tacos with pickled onions, we had a few rounds of cava. After lunch, full of delicious pork and pink bubbly, we felt braver, looser, ready to take on Can Paixano like a local.

Our inhibitions covered up with our lunch rounds, we entered the dark hole in the wall. It was just a little after 1:30 pm on a Monday, and this place was freaking packed. Here are the rules: no tables, standing room only; you must order two appetizers with your drinks; and there is little to no English. We weaved our way up to the bar and ordered our first glasses, with some Manchego cheese and charcuterie meats. We downed glass after glass; white cava, rose cava…we tried it all. Each glass was only like 1.50 euro. You could literally FEEL the energy in the room…everyone buzzed on this delicious, happy bubbly. It was one of those pure, raw travel moments where you feel like you are a part of something bigger than yourself. Like you are swept up in another world and are looking at yourself experiencing it from outside your body. The dark bar, shielding us from Spain's intense September sun. The gorgeous Castilian language, of which I didn't understand a word. The fresh and crispy pink cava. The heightened energy field of people undefined on Spanish bubbly. I closed my eyes for a moment, in gratitude for this experience. I knew, even in my softened, intoxicated fuzziness that it was special. Where do these people work???? If this was Pennsylvania, there is no way in HELL that anyone would be in a cava bar, so full you are shoulder to shoulder, in the middle of an afternoon on a Monday. Just no way. God, do I love me some culture!

Needless to say, I was TRASHED on cava, before it was even 4 pm. We left Can Paixano and made our way up to Passeig de Gràcia, one of the most famous high-end shopping boulevards in Barcelona. We stumbled through Hermès, Prada, and finally landed in Gucci, carrying on the whole way. In Gucci, they served us MORE cava. Trenton tried on a gazillion outfits and ended up spending a cool grand on a Gucci sweatsuit. I had the time of my life.

THE GRAYS

It was a Monday morning, late in October. I sat in the middle of my bedroom, on the floor, angrily ripping all the pictures off my vision board. I tore EVERY SINGLE ONE off and stuffed them in an envelope that contained a beautiful card with Buddha on the front, the expensive foiled kind you can buy at Barnes and Noble. I had purchased this card last April, and in it I had written this heartfelt letter to the universe with all my hopes and dreams. To hell with the universe. Screw vision boards. I shoved the envelope full of my vision board pics and letter in one of my old journals and slammed it shut in a drawer. Next, I took EVERY SINGLE self-development, universe loving, quantum physics exploring, food planning book off every shelf in my house, packed them up, and delivered them to the Good Will. I was DONE. I was done asking the universe for help, asking for guidance from guardian angels, reading about people's miraculous moments where they were guided on a different path. I was done trying out a different food plan to lose the weight that never seems to stay away for long (Whole 30, Keto, South Beach, Paleo, Skinny Bitch)…you name it, I've read it all, done it all, and all I can say is THE HELL WITH IT ALL. The programs I've bought, the podcasts I've listened to, the money wasted, the time, the emotion, etc., all because I thought (???) I was taking inspired action(???) (And screw THAT, too) to become a better version of me, to live a happier life, and to inspire others to do the same. After many years of this route, and a FULL month of working on myself from the time I woke up 'til I went to sleep…journaling, reading, working through programs…I felt I was further way from co-creating with the universe (again, the hell with that) than ever before. I was angry, hurt, and so sad. I truly wanted to believe in the magic of the universe, the comfort of a guardian angel, the positive momentum of a gratitude list. But all around me was a deafening silence. I felt locked away behind many, many gray, cold cement blocks. And here I was again, that little girl of 5 or 6, clutching a handful of forget-me-nots that were never acknowledged by the universe.

My sabbatical was supposed to be full of French and art classes, travel, relaxation, self-development, health, and growth. I had envisioned myself enjoying my home in a way that I never get to…by myself and perfectly cleaned. I dreamed that after everyone got off to work and school, that I would be able to sit in my quiet, clean house that I finally was able to organize. I'd play Mozart, burn my Free People candle, and work on my book and enhancing my curriculum at school. I'd happily journal my way through all the life enhancing programs I had dropped money on…Oh! The luxury of time that I've never had! Time to work out; time to make myself lunch; time to walk my property and watch the seasons change. My life has been, for the past 20 years, full blown chaos and grind. To have TIME, a tranquil clean space, days filled with beautiful activities…

The reality?? My house is a construction zone. We decided to remodel our daughters' bathroom. We had been buying marble for almost a year so we could afford to do this bathroom exactly as we had envisioned. My husband planned to do the bulk of the work while I was in Florence in September, since he knows I'm both a micromanager and a spaz when it comes to "trying" to keep our house clean. A few days before I left for Italy, I came home from Giant Eagle to a toilet being thrown out of my front door, with pieces of shower surround soon to follow. And as with most reno projects, the timeline you plan is never what actually happens. So a month and a half later, I'm existing in a house all day where every single surface is covered with drywall dust, no matter how many times I sweep or wipe them clean. There's a new pedestal sink along with a toilet lid randomly sitting in my kitchen. My cats, who are both indoor and outdoor cats, are constantly dragging mulch... and ticks because it's fall...through the house. You can see my fingerprints swirled into the dust on the mousepad of my laptop, even though I clean it off constantly. Please don't get me wrong; I am so grateful for the remodel, and I'm so blessed to have a husband who is so skilled to be able to do this, but my daily space I was living in was NOT what I had planned. My physical life chaos, coupled with the abandonments I felt with my spiritual work and the extreme financial stress in planning for my next travel class, was a recipe for a meltdown. It was a tantrum of grand proportions, that lasted a whole weekend. I yelled, cried, questioned the purpose of life, cried some more, got super pissed, then it ended with me packing all my spiritual shit up and getting it out of my house. My husband said at least I wasn't a poet, since they live in the headspace I was currently in all the time...

I spent the next couple of weeks in turmoil. I experienced every kind of despair...and was definitely feeling sorry for myself, at first. An interesting thing transpired out of this dramatic month. When I was at a loss for what I was feeling and breaking down in tears right and left, it was my husband who was there to pick me up. Now, some of you might be thinking why is this unusual for a husband to do for his wife? It's not, really, but in my situation, it was. Where I am very social and have a NEED to connect to others and engage with friends, my husband does not. It's not that he isn't sweet and caring (he actually is the SWEETEST), but he is a man of few words and not one to engage in major chatty conversations. He prefers to be alone, reading, to hanging out with people at happy hour. We know these differences in each other and respect them, so in all honesty, we really just don't talk all that much. I also am fiercely independent and am very bad at asking for help. After being married for 24 years, we have certainly fallen into a comfortable pattern of us just doing our own thing and being our own people.

As I stood in the hallway in front of our bedroom, carrying on like a two year old about tearing apart my vision board and how DUMB the universe is, he provided me with a constant stream of wisdom, encouragement, and support. I was taken aback with how well he understood how I was feeling, and how unbelievably patient he was with my bratty behavior. *Another gift from the universe.* It wasn't until after I had time to process my sabbatical that I saw this gift, the gift of my quiet husband knowing me on a deeper level that I had ever expected. A million thank you's to him will never be enough for his emotional and financial support of my sabbatical whim.

After the storm of my breakdown had cleared, instead of walking around my house feeling overwhelmed and angry, I looked deep to find what I love about European culture, and I brought that to my daily life to carry me through this tumultuous semester. I took myself on a café crawl around Pittsburgh. Each week that I had left before my next trip, I chose a different café that had a European vibe to it, and I would spend the day there. I would write, study my French and art, drink hot chocolate and eat croissants, enjoy charcuterie boards with champagne for lunch, and people watch. I went to little art galleries and hole in the wall bookstores. The Saturday before I left for Québec, I spent the day in the Strip District in Pittsburgh with my friend Greg. As a Pittsburgh native, I never chose to really investigate my own city for what it had to offer. The Strip is a vibrant, eclectic neighborhood full of ethnic food shops, street vendors, classic Italian style eateries, little boutiques, and converted warehouses. Even though it was a cold brisk November day, the Strip was bustling with people and smells of kettle corn, hot sausage and pierogies, and Italian ladylocks. A little gem, right in my hometown. The scene of the dismantling of my vision board and shipping my self-help book collection off to Good Will seemed far away from me, here amidst the dried lavender in Roxanne's Dried Flowers and warm rich chocolate in Mon Aimee Chocolat. I would be leaving for Québec City in the morning.

QUÉBEC CITY

There-in the Château Frontenac, sipping vodka Pur in Bar 1608, watching the snowflakes fall like sugar from the sky over the St. Lawrence, smelling like Labo's Rose 31.

There-on Rue du Trésor, Artist's Alley, discussing local art en français, with a beautiful bohemian man who wore high boots and a ponytail.

There-in Café La Maison Smith-burying myself in the most delicious hot chocolate and croissant, alone with my gratitude.

There-in the middle of the woods with snowdrifts and fir trees as far as the eye can see, breathing in the sharp cold air, while my numb hands grip the bar of the dog sled-gliding over the icy trail deep in the Québec countryside.

There-in La Galerie d'art Beauchamp, sitting quietly in the gallery, surrounded by modern pieces juxtaposed against original brick-walled rooms-feeling the electricity, yet stillness, of this rich contrast which is so comfortable to me.

There-in snowbanks taller than me, digging and playing in the snow with my students, remembering what it's like to just BE.

There-in a city where people can flow in and out of French and English as fluid as my breath…

There-at the top of the Escalier Casse-Cou, looking down on the Petit Champlain, brimming with boutiques and restaurants that welcome with their artsy storefronts, lovelier than a postcard.

It is HERE, in Québec City, that I first fell in love, hard, with a place. And like any first love, there is a special little space carved out in the puzzle of ME where Québec fits. And, like any best love affair, there is no true end in the heart. A thousand visits will never be enough.

"Forgiveness is the smell that lavender gives out when you tread on it." Mark Twain

Québec City, November 2019

Traveling to, talking about traveling to, and planning travel to France, Italy, and Québec City is like listening to Radiohead for me. It's like that moment when I hear Thom Yorke's unforgettable voice swirled with Radiohead's signature hypnotic music…my whole self immediately opens up-expands-and I get this instant rush. I feel alive, free, connected, enveloped in emotion so intense, yet relaxed at the same time. That's what seeing the Eiffel Tower rise up suddenly on a side street, drinking a perfect bowl of chocolat chaud at Québec City's quirky café Cochon Dingue, watching the world go by as I sip rosé in a Parisian café, or coming face to face with Michelangelo's *David* makes me feel. EVERY. SINGLE. TIME. A feeling so personal that I want to keep it secret, yet a high so great I want to share it with the world. And to think that there actually was a time, not that long ago, that I didn't even know this part of me existed…

I have always, for as long as I can think back, been drawn to the French culture, language, architecture, gardens, style, fashion…you name it. But it was always just a little dream that I kept locked away in my heart. I was a small-town girl from a middle-class family that lived on a family farm. I didn't even see the ocean until I was in college. The extent of a family vacation was to go to neighboring Ohio to visit Sea World, just for the day. While my childhood was truly great and my family loving and supportive, we just didn't DO things like travel, or even talk about that kind of stuff like it was a possibility.

When it came time to choose a career, it really was a no brainer for me to study French and English secondary education (I was going to be a FRENCH TEACHER!!!!) But somehow, I still blocked out the part about traveling??? It was so NOT a part of my life that I couldn't even frame that idea in my brain.

So I got really good at French grammar, really really good at verb conjugations and writing, and kinda skated by in the rest (um...like speaking and listening, anyone??? Actual live communication with a human being??) I had started to build a fear around those things because they were unknowable to me.

These thoughts and memories overwhelmed my mind as I walked the mile trek to my French immersion school, Québec Monde École de Français. As I walked along the St. Lawrence river from the Petit Champlain to St. Roch, I suddenly felt like it was the summer of 1991.

I had just finished up my sophomore year at Clarion University. I somehow let my French professor talk me into participating in a French immersion program in Québec. I didn't realize it then because I was so overwhelmed with this experience, but that summer of '91 was when my eternal love for Québec began…and my desire to travel was born.

I stopped for a moment in my walk and looked across the river, not really seeing the Lévis shore on the other side, but instead seeing the memories of my first real travel experience. I saw myself standing at the top of the Casse-Cou steps for the first time looking at the postcard perfect street below me, with all of the quaint boutiques and inviting cafés. I saw myself winding through the cobblestone streets, finding magic around every corner. I saw myself at my first art gallery, Galerie Le Chien d'Or. Dancing at the L'Utrek, the club that was on campus, counting down into the use of ALL French with the other students just like it was New Year's Eve…I let all of these images wash over me, remembering the FEAR. Remembering how far I've come from that scared 20-year-old girl. Remembering that first drive to Québec City with my parents who dropped me off. A drive that I now take every year, bringing hundreds of my own students here to experience this enchanted city.

I drew in a sharp breath against the cold November air and buried my face further in my plaid scarf, inhaling the Le Labo's Rose 31. This was, without question, my chosen Québec scent, as Rose 31 was the scent that permeated the Château Frontenac. The spicy, woodsy, rose essence always makes me feel the calm, luxurious hush that I experience each time I enter a room at the Château, one of the most photographed hotels in the world, where I stay with my students each winter. Lost in my reverie of past Québec trips, the cold air brought me back to thinking about my first French class in 25 years.

During that summer of 1991, I sold myself short. I let FEAR win. Because of strong written and grammar skills, I tested into the second highest level of the program. However, my friends from Pennsylvania tested into the middle levels. I was NOT about to struggle through this experience by myself. NO WAY. So I faked like I didn't understand what was going on so I could get moved down to the level with my friends. Not only was I now comfortable because I was with people I knew, but I was also extremely comfortable with the material. It was easy for me. I already knew it. Certainly, no growing or expanding going on there. But I sure did have one hell of a time.

I resumed my walk to class. As I walked, I allowed myself to feel these old fears AND all my current fears. I let myself feel the emotional turmoil, the disappointments, my past failures, and the stress of the month and a half leading up to this trip. But I didn't let them take residence in my body. It was time to let go. Right there at the St. Lawrence River, I forgave them. I forgave myself. I forgave that 20-year-old girl from '91. I forgave my ego for protecting me.

I had class from 9-12:30 every day. My professor's name was Sylvie. I loved her on sight. She was dressed in baggy Levis with a tucked in flannel shirt, a gray fleece ear band wrapped around her gray straight hair, her bangs resting over top of the band. She was no nonsense, but warm. Because it was an immersion school, there was NO English. We began introducing ourselves in French, and from there our week of classes took form. As I spoke, she wrote down errors. From those errors, our lessons were built. It was a very organic and personalized process. She corrected every grammatical and pronunciation error and taught me new vocabulary and structures. I was in heaven. I let go of every ounce of self-protection and allowed her to teach me. To be able to discuss the imparfait tense in French with an expert connected with the super nerdy side of me that simply adores grammar, while refueling my passion for the humanities, for learning. I fell in love a little with Sylvie, as I tend to do with anyone who takes up residence in my soul.

Every day at 10:30 we had a "pause," a little break. I would go next door to this charming chocolatier called *Champagne Chocolatier.* It had a Spanish vibe to it, with brightly colored tables and yellow, orange, and blue mosaic décor. I always ordered a dark chocolat chaud and a trois chocolats (3 chocolates) muffin. I sat in the window seat and watched the snowflakes tumble together from the sky.

That first day of class Sylvie looked at my cute leopard Steve Madden combat boots with disdain and asked me if I had snow boots. I told her these were my only boots, as I thought they were sufficient for walking in a little November snow. Sylvie told me that Québec was bracing for its first big snow of the year that night, at least a foot and a half!!!!

I really can't think of anything else that makes me feel little kid excitement more than a good snowstorm-not Christmas morning, birthday cakes, or beach vacations. Perhaps it's the teacher in me; there is NOTHING like anticipating a snow day!!! I've seen Québec City in all of its winter splendor for many years, but this would be my first time experiencing their first huge snowstorm of the season!

So, after class, I headed to the Upper Town, to Rue St. Jean, to shop for winter boots. Rue St. Jean is one of the main shopping streets in Vieux Québec. It is lined with boutiques, well-known stores like Lush, a department store called Simon's, and many cafés and restaurants. Such a modern, chic shopping area located in bucolic stone historical buildings creates a hip, eclectic vibe. I easily found Columbia snow boots, then spent the rest of the afternoon leisurely visiting boutiques. Because of the anticipation of the winter weather, I was feeling especially festive and popped into *3 Poules*, a rustic-chic home boutique. With its high, stark, white-washed brick walls, greenery, and woven bohemian decor, I felt like I was in HGTV's Joanna Gaines' home. I settled on a simple glass bulb shaped ornament with a piece of pine inside.

Before I headed back to my Auberge to do my homework, I went to *Le Casse-Crêpe Breton*. I've been here numerous times, but I'm usually rushed because I'm traveling with my students. I chose a window seat, where I could look out and see that the snow was just lightly starting to fall. I ordered a dry white wine from Spain and a crêpe filled with fresh strawberries and freshly made whipped cream. I ate slowly, thinking that there really isn't anything more luxurious than fresh whipped cream. I ordered another glass of wine. I thought about last month, and how angry I was at the universe and myself. I wondered, for a moment, if I needed to have those breakdowns to release old emotions and beliefs, to make room for new. I shrugged. Right now, at this moment at least, all I felt was peace, calm, and contentment.

I woke up the next morning in the middle of a snow globe. It was still early in the morning when I headed out, so many of the streets and sidewalks had not been touched. There was hardly anyone around. I trudged through the Place-Royale, the site of the first French settlement in North America, making my own path as I walked. I went into Café La Maison Smith and set myself up at the bar at the windows, overlooking the square. With my chocolat chaud and quiche végétarienne, I gazed out at the Notre-Dame-des-Victoires, the oldest stone church in North America. Right beside the church, I noticed that some men were getting ready to put up the largest live Christmas tree I had ever seen! I was mesmerized by the scene…the snow that was past my ankles; the decadent hot chocolate swirled with cream; the men erecting the Christmas tree; I felt suspended inside beauty- riding inside a champagne bubble-rising to the top then exploding with all the things golden, sweet, celebratory, delicate, and captivating. I will never forget this moment.

Each morning I would walk the mile in the cold and snow to my school and then walk a mile back to the Auberge St. Pierre, where I was staying. In the mornings, I walked brusquely along the river, grateful to have the walk to clear my mind and burn off all the chocolat chaud, croissants, and French onion soup I was enjoying. On the way back though, I would take my time. I always chose to walk inward along Rue St. Paul. I strolled slowly, stopping at each store front, daydreaming in front of the antiques' displays, the collectors' items, and the art galleries…Oh!!! The galleries…

Les Galeries Beauchamp

I first fell in love with the Beauchamp Galleries a few summers ago, when I was visiting Québec with Michael and Trenton. The first afternoon there, we went down to the lower town and found ourselves among art gallery after art gallery, all owned by the Beauchamp family. To the left upon entering 10 du Sault-au-Matelot, was a gigantic canvas on display-a mixed media of Twiggy, Picasso, Guernica, and the quote "Art is a lie that makes us realize the truth" in a bright pink stripe. For reasons unknown, as it usually is when art, music, or literature grab our heart, I was so moved I felt like crying. The owner, Vincent Beauchamp, was amused by my emotion and exuberance over the piece, his galleries, art in general, and speaking French. I immediately adored him. Because of Vincent, I was able to believe I could own original art; and with a payment plan set up, I bought that piece. I told Vincent that I would come work for him immediately. He laughed and said I was welcome anytime. We kept in touch as I made my payments on my acquisition. Fast forward to my sabbatical: as part of my learning experience in Québec City, I e-mailed Vincent about interning in his art gallery. He graciously accepted my request, and one of my days in Québec was spent with his daughter Maude.

Maude is a beautiful blond with sparkling eyes, an even sparklier personality, and a quick smile. She was young-18 I found out- but mature beyond her years. Her warmth spilled out of her, and we connected immediately. Maude led me around the galleries, teaching me about the artists, their works, what made them unique, and the mediums the artists used. All in French. HOW IS THIS MY LIFE. I was literally on cloud 9...being led around a stunning art gallery, discussing the works in French. At one point, I stopped and said to Maude, "You must LOVE your job." "Oh yes," she said. After a second, she added, "I work in beauty, and I sell beauty." These words gripped my heart.

One piece in particular caught my attention, a piece by local artist Patrick Pépin. It was inspired by the Sagrada Familia in Barcelona and titled as such. Since I had just been to Barcelona for the first time a few months prior, the title grabbed me. This modern, bright composition instantly felt as though I was floating in a sea of stained glass: liquid color with sharp angled edges. I knew this would be hanging in my house sometime soon. Maude and I put on our coats and gloves to go across the street to visit their other galleries. As we were headed out the door, linked arm in arm to hold each other up on the icy streets, Maude stopped to talk to a tall, thin gentleman wearing a newsboy hat who had just come in. After kissing him on both cheeks, she said, "Patrick, this is Heidi. She is a friend of my father's from the United States. We were just talking about you! She is buying your Sagrada Familia #90 work!" Oh. My. God. Here I was, face to face with a well-known artist, meeting him like it was an everyday occurrence. Patrick smiled warmly and asked me about my visit to

Québec. We chatted for a few moments in French about his work, and he pointed out a few details on the piece I was buying. Like how on the back of every one of his works is the exact photograph for his inspiration. My heart was racing the whole time. OH MY WHEN THE STARS ALIGN, THEY REALLY ALIGN.

Mentally exhausted from a full day of class and discussing art in French, I decided to head to the Upper Town to Bar 1608 in the Château Frontenac to sit in my happiness and indulge in a little celebration. The Frontenac is ICONIC Québec City, and luxury at its finest. Although I stay here every year with my students, I rarely get to enjoy the other aspects of the hotel, like the bars and boutiques. As I walked through the lobby down the main hall towards Bar 1608, I stopped short, as the entire hallway was lined with Christmas trees all lit up, at least 20 of them! As I was admiring them (and of course, taking pictures!!) a gentleman from the hotel came up and asked me in French if I liked the trees. After telling him how gorgeous they were and how fortunate I was that I got to see them, he told me to stick around, as they were having their annual Christmas tree decorating party that evening! He said that each of the trees was going to be decorated by a local business, who had decided on a theme for their tree. I couldn't believe my luck, that I had stumbled upon yet another fairytale moment.

I closed my eyes in Bar 1608 for a moment, simply allowing the spontaneous feeling from within myself that had just bubbled up flow. So. Much. Gratitude. I ordered a cheese board and champagne. A hefty price tag no doubt, but I was treating myself! My board contained three different types of cheeses from goat, sheep, and cow's milk, red grapes, figs, walnuts, and a beautiful raspberry jam swirl. When I finished, I went back out to the lobby and hallway, where the decorating party was in full swing! There was music, an open bar, and much joy as the businesses decorated their trees. I observed from the side and let the gaiety of the moment fill me-fill me with everything pink and glittery and warm and fuzzy.

Sometimes a fairy-tale rescue is not from a knight in shining armor; sometimes it's a city. And that's the magic of Québec.

"While most of the time she was in good spirits, on occasion it all turned to one great desert. At these times, Wren would find a need to call upon the moondragon and go off reminding herself of all the magic in the world." -Seth Pitt, artist

"For my part I know nothing with any certainty, but the sight of the stars makes me dream." -Vincent van Gogh

St. Rémy de Provence, France, 2017

We should have known we were headed for magic. Two gypsy women appeared out of nowhere, on a dirt road before an expanse of field. Their skin was brown and leathery from the sun, their breasts hanging low and barely covered by the sheer material of their dress. In Thelma and Louise style, with big sunglasses and silk scarves purchased in Nice, my two girlfriends and I had rented a car in the South of France and were driving through Aix-en-Provence for a one-night stay in the small town of St. Rémy. We had been driving, almost comically, literally round and round in one of France's numerous roundabouts, and we couldn't seem to get off the right way to our hotel. As startled as we were by being stopped by these French gypsies, the women pointed us in the right direction that led us down a road lined with Plane trees on either side.

We spent the evening strolling through the cobblestone streets and 14th century stone wall remains, sampling ice cream and finding the birthplace of Nostradamus. We finally found ourselves in a lovely open square, where we dined on lemon sugar crêpes washed down with bottle after bottle of Mas de Bourgonnier wine, the most delicious wine I've ever had.

Perhaps it was breathing in the same air that Vincent van Gogh had as he painted his most famous works.

Perhaps it was the delightful view of the twinkling stars that I could catch through the trees as we sat in the outdoor café.

Perhaps it was the wine itself.

But the for the first time in my 40 some years, the line between dreams and reality was blurred-

I no longer was the woman who had never really left her small hometown in Pennsylvania because, well, she just didn't.

I no longer was the woman who dreamed endlessly of the lavender fields of Provence while being seduced by the French language.

Just like that, I had walked inside my dreams.

So somewhere along Autoroute 7, perhaps at the roundabout where the gypsies were, my energy had shifted. And in that shift flowed a gratitude that was so overwhelming, it swirled around me like Van Gogh's sky and took my breath away.

Montpellier, France

December 2019

I immediately longed for the warmth of my Québec professor Sylvie. It was 8 am on Monday, December 9, and I had just arrived at the Institut Linguistique Adenet (I'll refer to my school as ILA from here on out) in the South of France. After my friendly "Bonjour, Madame! Je suis ici pour mon orientation" was met with an icy half smile and a point towards a little room off to the side, I wondered if I had made a mistake. This was my last trip of my sabbatical, and my first time being in a group class. Trying not to feel disappointed, I turned to the other two people in the little conference room. The first guy, older than me, introduced himself as a geography professor from Michigan. The other was a much younger man, a student from Germany. After meeting them, I had my second moment of questioning my choice to come here. Both men were complete beginners with the French language, and I was here in the same orientation…did I really mess up my placement exam THAT BAD???

I had taken the placement exam for ILA in a rush, after I had received an urgent e-mail from them reminding me that they could not complete my registration because I had not taken the exam to determine my level. Shit. Between my trip to Québec and cleaning up the post construction mess at my house to host Thanksgiving, I had completely forgotten. I barely had my eyes open yet when I had received this e-mail; I hurriedly clicked the link that said *START TEST*. Immediately I regretted that hasty decision, as I watched a 100-question exam download. *100 questions.* There was no turning back now; I had one shot after opening the link. I sleepily stumbled through the questions. I knew it wasn't my best work…but a class with people who didn't know how to say "my name is?" My fears were laid to rest, though, when after a brief general orientation, we were all taken to different classrooms.

Because this is a language institute, people from all over the world come here to learn French. Some people had been there for six weeks, and some, like me, for just this week. However, the class I entered seemed to have been together for quite some time. I was the only newbie. I was still kind of sweating after narrowly escaping the thought of being with beginners. Fabrice, my professor, was about my age (maybe 46?? 47??) and was a native French man. He was friendly (MUCH friendlier than the women at the reception desk) and welcomed me and suggested everyone in the class introduce themselves, in French, starting with me. I had no idea what I was even walking into, so I didn't want to do the basic name, age, occupation, etc. type of intro. So I launched into this big presentation on what I had been doing during my sabbatical and why I was there. When I finished, everyone was just silent. Fabrice said, in French of course, "Well! That was quite the intro! Let's continue with everyone else!" I again was uncomfortable, AGAIN kicking myself for taking a group class. I guess, though, it turned out that I had taken my prof aback a little with all of my detail, and during our break, he asked me if I wanted to move up a level. I politely declined, as they were hot and heavy in the middle of the subjunctive tense, which I hadn't done since high school. I needed the review. And while his offer to advance me fed my ego, I had to remember that the WHOLE POINT of me taking classes was to check my ego and fear at the door, so I could be open to my weaknesses and learn.

In my class was Heath, a human rights activist from Australia; three biomedical engineers from Atlanta, Georgia; and several young people from Columbia and Switzerland. I was in awe of Heath and the three from Atlanta. These were adults, like me, who were established in their careers. They were all sent here from their companies to learn French. The Atlanta Georgia crew was headed to Africa to do research; and Heath, who had just been in Somalia, was also headed back to Africa to assist with the Peace Corps. I couldn't wrap my mind around the true globalization that went on outside of my little town in Pennsylvania, where it seemed like all anyone in Cranberry Township cared about was talking about what they bought at Home Goods over the weekend.

We had class every day from 9am-12:30 pm, which consisted of grammar and writing. It was really like sitting in any classroom, with notes, exercises that we completed together, and partner conversations. The subjunctive, the superlative with both adverbs and adjectives, and which prepositions to use after an infinitive made up our lessons. *God, how I adore grammar!*

It struck me that everyone's attitudes, although they had chosen to be here, were just like any typical student. There was a general air of "over it" throughout since this was the last week of class before Christmas break. And, in true teacher fashion, our prof brought in games, a movie, and a treat of *chouquettes*, little balls of puff pastry with sugar on them that resembled donut holes, on our last day of class. We even played Kahoot!, which is a favorite of my middle school students back in the USA. Our Kahoot! topic? French culture. And guess who won Kahoot!? The American from Butler County, Pennsylvania. Yours truly.

My afternoon class was from 1:15 pm to 4 and was strictly conversation and listening. I expected to reconvene in the afternoon with Fabrice and the rest of my morning classmates. To my discomfort, I entered a room with ALL unfamiliar faces, and a different prof. My conversation teacher's name was Laure. She was very animated, young, and smoked a lot. I looked around the room. I could have been EVERYONE'S mom there. Everyone's. Including my teacher. Most of the students in my class were from Columbia. They spoke rapid fire Spanish to each other (even though we had signed an agreement to ONLY use French) and then spoke rapid fire French that I could NOT understand because it still sounded like rapid fire Spanish. They were also late to class EVERY DAY. The girls spent their time rolling their eyes and tapping away on their cell phones with their long, fake nails, while our teacher had us role play and initiate awkward conversations. The only thing that kept me from walking out was Thomas, a good-natured boy from Australia, who wore too short sweatpants every day and was obsessed with Star Wars. And Julian, the only male in the young Columbian posse. If I'm being completely honest here, I was crushing on Julian. He was slight, quiet, always had a gray scarf loosely tied around his neck and wore artsy black rimmed glasses. He spoke French so gorgeously, with such poise and personality, that I found myself hanging on his every French word. He was beautiful. Obviously, the other Columbian females in the class thought so, too, as they giggled and snapped their gum loudly every time Julian spoke.

As with my other travels, the first thing that I need to do when I arrive somewhere is settle into some kind of routine immediately. Where some people find the idea of an unexplored foreign city with no itinerary freeing and exciting, I find it panic-inducing and incredibly scary. A routine was the only way that I held onto that imaginary thread of control. So my first day in Montpellier, I set out to find the boulangerie where I'd have my pain au chocolat and chocolat chaud every day. I first tried a croissant at Ortholan, which was recommended to me by the front desk at my hotel and was conveniently located on the top of the street where my school was. Although the croissant WAS delicious, they did not have hot chocolate AND the people who worked there were cold and indifferent. Not how I needed to start my French day. I moved on down the street to a cute little artisan boulanger with a bright orange awning—Maison Teissier. After seeing chocolat chaud on the menu and being waited on by a warm grandmotherly type, I knew this was it. Every morning, I would take a brisk walk past Les Halles Castellane, Montpellier's covered marketplace. After taking in the stalls of brightly colored fresh fruits and veggies, cheese, fresh pasta, flowers, fish, I would turn the corner to Maison Teissier and order my pain au chocolat and chocolat chaud to go. I would eat my croissant on the way to class, like I saw the other university students doing, brushing the inevitable croissant crumbs (*les miettes*) from their scarves as they hurried to their class. After my morning class, I stopped every day at the Bagel Corner, which was at the top of Rue Grand Jean Moulin, where ILA was. I LOVED Bagel Corner. Every day I got a fresh bagel with herbed cream cheese, tons of fresh veggies, avocado, and a little scoop of fried onions…freaking DELICIOUS… and cheap! The same girl waited on me every day, and by the end of the week knew my order and my name. After my afternoon class, I tried to complete my homework. Then I headed out for happy hour and exploring Montpellier with my friend Beth, who had joined me part way through my week in the South of France.

Beth is a more recent friend in my world. Her realness, her ability to make me laugh out loud, her fierce pride of her kids but no bullshit attitude of calling them out when they are in the wrong, her intelligence, her sense of FUN, has cemented a relationship that I look forward to embracing for years to come. Because of Beth's independent nature, she was a perfect person to join me in France. She was content to explore Montpellier on her own while I was in class. Then we would meet up for the evening for dinner and more exploring after I had finished my homework. In addition to loving her independent and easy-going attitude, I also loved that we have the tendency to get ourselves into some adventures when together…

The Brits

I woke up to a text from Beth at a little after 8 am, asking me if I was up. Shit!! I jumped out of bed and IMMEDIATELY regretted that. I had to be in class by 9, and I was in the full throes of feeling all the famous Montpellier rosé I drank last night. My head was pounding, mouth dry as a desert, dizzy, shaking… all I wanted to do was crawl -literally crawl- back into my nice hotel bed in Montpellier. But this was my second to last day of class. I had a verb test today and a speaking assessment. I HAD TO GO. I stood in a hot shower, dressed, and drug myself to get my daily croissant. The fresh air definitely helped clear the fuzzy feeling from my head a little. I sat on the edge of the fountain on Rue Grand Jean Moulin, downing my croissant in three bites, desperately trying to calm my post rosé binge shakes with some fat and carbs. As I took in some deep breaths of fresh air and tried to pull myself together before I went into class, I checked my phone to look at the pictures of last night.

Yesterday afternoon started off innocently enough. Beth and I went to Beer O'Clock on Rue en Gondeau for an early *Apéro* (French Happy Hour). Beer O'Clock is a nontouristy craft beer and wine bar off a little side street in Montpellier's historical center. There was no one in the bar when we got there, as it was early for French people to be out at Apéro. With glasses of Mas Rouge rosé and the loveliest charcuterie board with cheese and meat fresh from Halles Castellane, Montpellier's food market, Beth and I relaxed into the slower paced deliciousness of the South of France. As one glass of wine faded into another, more people came in, starting their own Apéro. We didn't notice the four gentlemen sitting at a table behind us. They must have overheard us talking, because all of a sudden, the oldest in the group, probably in his 50's, came over to us and said, "Thank God! I finally hear English!" He got in between our bar stools, lightly draped an arm over both of us, and continued. "So nice to see two beautiful women speaking English! Hi, my name is Rye." (Actually, I later realized that his name is RAY, and it just sounded like RYE because of his heavy British accent). Beth and I were friendly and polite, while definitely sending the message that we were NOT interested in being hit on by guys in Beer O'Clock. Rye (Ray) went back to his friends after a few guarded moments of pleasantries. As Beth and I moved onto another glass of rosé, Ray was back. Slightly annoyed with his presence again, we politely let him tell us his story. He and his three friends were the last of a group of British police officers who had taken a minivacation together from England to Montpellier. Because of the French strikes, their flights kept getting cancelled. They had come to Beer O'Clock, dragging their luggage, no hotel, hoping to make a plan over a few craft beers. I glanced behind Ray, to his three other colleagues, whom I had not paid attention to until now. Maybe it was the several glasses of wine, or Ray's stressful story, but somehow we became a group of six. There was Ray, their sweet, anxious leader; Liam, tall with a pleasant, open face and a most charming personality; Max, the youngest of the group (late 20's?), with a ripped physique, sharp wit, and quick smile; and Ethan, a beautiful man with a chiseled, model worthy face and gentle demeanor. They were all members of the British police force. And just like that, this group of complete strangers became a group of friends for the evening, embracing the night out, with only the fact that we all spoke English in a foreign country binding us together. The glasses of wine became bottles. We talked comfortably and respectfully about politics…Trump as our President and their Prime Minister Boris Johnson. We discussed the possibility of Brexit, the UK leaving the European Union (which became official on January 31, 2020). Max laughed over the stereotype of the American female being attracted to the British accent---he made me say over and over in a Valley Girl accent—OH MA GAWD… ARE YOU BRITISH??

By now, Beer O'Clock was BUMPIN', and they were setting up an improv show in the back of the bar where we were sitting. And like anytime that you've been drinking for a long time, we suddenly found ourselves in the middle of a different environment. We were bottles and bottles of wine in, among French people who were just getting started, and people trying to enjoy a French improv show. We had become the loud English speakers who were disrupting the show, and we were politely asked to leave. Unfazed…and unaware of how obnoxious our group of six had become, we happily stumbled through the streets of Montpellier, looking for our next bar, the Brits' suitcases bumping behind us. We stopped at Le Yams, an outdoor café in La Place de la Comédie, which was right next to our hotel. More bottles of wine were ordered. Almost immediately a drinking game was started---NEVER HAVE I EVER--- and without hesitation, we went right for everyone's juiciest secrets, no warmup necessary. Round after round, we got louder, spicier, and more ridiculous, until...the waiter THERE asked us to leave! Giggling like crazy and leaning on one another, we crossed the square to stand in line at the walk-up McDonalds window. After I ordered my fries to go, I had a feeling of pure happiness, freedom. I looked around at my new group of friends, bonded together by language, a shared experience, and chance. When I had originally started planning my solo travels, I dreamed of an unforgettable European adventure. Something that wasn't a part of my classes. Something cultural, adult, and wildly fun. I dreamed of maybe hitting a dance club during my weekend in Barcelona, or vibing at Paris' Hôtel Costes with a cool mixed drink. Getting kicked out of two bars with four police officers from England, playing *Never Have I Ever* in the South of France like a bunch of high schoolers in someone's basement, was definitely NOT on my radar. But it was perfect. And I learned again...the universe delivers something even better than your dreams, in a way you can never plan out.

I took one last look at our group picture from last

night, then headed into my class. Not only was I hungover, but I hadn't studied at all for my quiz. I could not believe my eyes when my prof handed out our tests. How is this my lucky day?? EVERY SINGLE VERB ON IT was a verb that I teach my French 2 classes. I knew these verbs inside and out. I was the first one done. And I got 100 percent. And the night with the Brits??? 100 percent worth it.

RACLETTE

Beth and I decided to visit the European Christmas market our last night in Montpellier. It was mid-December, so the Christmas season was in full swing in France. I was so excited to experience this cultural phenomenon firsthand. Over the years during the Christmas season in my classroom, I've taught about Noël in France, without actually experiencing it myself. I've taught about the *Santons* from the South of France (the nativity figurines), the *Treize Desserts* (13 desserts), and *le jour de Saint Nicholas*. Now here I was, in the South of France during Christmas time. I had my phone fully charged ready to capture every aspect of the Christmas market to document for my students.

The Christmas market, called Les Hivernales, was held off the Place de la Comédie, right past the 30 foot high glittering globe that I'm sure is an instagrammer's dream. By Pennsylvania standards, Montpellier was pretty warm, (like jean jacket and a scarf warm), but the locals were snugly dressed in winter gear and sipping the local mulled wine. The Christmas market was a beautiful walk, with local booths lining both sides. Beth and I were pleasantly surprised by the second booth where they were serving champagne in plastic champagne flutes (OHHHH how I love the French), which you could sip in a sophisticated fashion while shopping the local booths for the perfect Christmas present.

With champagne in hand, we strolled through the market, taking in all the sights and sounds of a holiday in another country. We looked at homemade jewelry, leather goods, and silk scarves. I found the booth that sold the Santons and took lots of pictures. I laughed out loud at the Yankee Candle booth. There were many people crowding around this booth, smelling scents like Buttercream and Home Sweet Home, scents that I could smell at my local mall. This must have been a special addition for the South of France because it was quite popular!! Beth and I moved on and found ourselves in front of a booth selling watches that were made of cork. Although I wasn't planning on buying anything, I was drawn to a feminine cork watch with a Tiffany blue face. For some reason, I had to have it. Although not a huge jewelry snob, I have three bracelets that I wear allllll of the time, that never come off, and two of them came from Tiffany's. I have a bracelet that Michael and Trenton gave me for being in their wedding, which stands for love and friendship. I have another one from Tiffany's with the iconic blue heart, which I purchased for myself that represents abundance. And then I have an all gold one that I bought in Florence, that stands for culture and travel. This watch seemed to fit in perfectly with my jewelry vibe. After our market purchases and champagne, we were ready to eat. Our original plan was to go to get crêpes at Le Kreisker, a café I could NOT get enough of while in Montpellier. Le Kreisker had the best crêpes I had EVER had, anywhere. My fave there had become the raspberry crêpe with fresh whipped cream…OMG. And crêpes with goat cheese. And honey. And pears. And OMG so delicious.

Anyway, on our way out of the Christmas market, we decided to check out the food there because EVERYONE SEEMED TO BE EATING SOMETHING. We were drawn to a stall that was kind of across from where I purchased my cork watch. It was decorated like a log cabin, with a huge block of cheese in the front. Upon closer inspection, there was a menu with a picture of steaming hot potatoes with melted cheese and all different accoutrements. And this, my friends, was my first introduction to RACLETTE.

As we looked over the menu, the woman working the booth asked if we had any questions. As I was unfamiliar with raclette, I asked her what it was. Raclette, apparently, (and after I had it rightfully so), was a super popular Swiss Alpine cow milk cheese that is heated and scraped off as it melts and is used as a topping. I was fascinated with watching the women working the booth scrape off the melted cheese block, top the orders, then put under a broiler to melt further. THIS WAS IT. Since I could speak French, I ordered while Beth got us another plastic flute of champagne. For under 20 euros, we stood at a side table in the outdoors at the Montpellier Christmas market and dined on potatoes with melted raclette and charcuterie with pickles, washed down with champagne. IT WAS HEAVEN. With the smells of roasted nuts and mulled wine as our backdrop, each forkful of raclette was pure BLISS. No amount of Vive le Vent (France's version of Jingle Bells) or pine tree smell could have put me more in the Christmas spirit than this raclette. HOW IS IT THAT THIS IS THE FIRST TIME THAT I HAVE HEARD OF THIS???? This is the kind of experience that I crave. The kind of thing to take back to my students. *The kind of cultural encounter that you cannot plan but that you just find yourself in the middle of, like it was just everyday life.* No need for crêpes tonight…full of warm potatoes covered in sumptuous raclette, Beth and I contentedly walked back to our hotel bar, where we finished the night with one last glass of Montpellier's rosé. In a peace that can only surround true friends, we sat, warmed by our raclette experience and pink bubbly, and said our own private good-byes to Montpellier, France.

"The purpose of art is washing the dust of daily life off our souls." Pablo Picasso

I giggled to myself as I stepped through the wide double windows out to our wrap-around balcony, remembering how Beth and I had booked this apartment in Le Marais, Paris.

We had gotten together at Beth's house to brainstorm/plan our France adventures. In true European fashion, we whipped up a spread to leisurely enjoy as we dreamed aloud: a charcuterie tray with meats, cheeses, raspberries paired with a buttery chardonnay or a zippy pino grigio, and potato chips with French onion dip paired with several bottles of prosecco. We did NOT start out with the intention of drinking all these bottles; but as the evening progressed, the bubbly, and our plans kept flowing. 5 bottles, a trip to a local bar for a vodka and club soda which neither of us could drink, and a two day hangover later, we had booked ourselves a luxury apartment in the third arrondissement, overlooking the gray zinc rooftops dotted with the iconic chimneypot clusters that create the skyline of Paris.

This was the end of my sabbatical, my last trip, my last stop. Unbeknownst to Beth, my wish to add a few days in Paris onto our Montpellier travels went beyond seeing the Eiffel Tower glittering at night or sipping wine in a local café. I <u>needed</u> to repair my relationship with Paris.

During the summer, my friends, my sister, and I had taken a two-week European vacation. We started and ended in Paris, and in between visited Capri and Positano in Italy; Bordeaux, France; and Mykonos and Santorini, Greece. The last day of our trip, we arrived in Paris from Santorini completely exhausted, both emotionally and physically. We had booked a room at the 5 star L'Hôtel, the last home of Oscar Wilde. I had the full intention of pampering myself in my own little slice of Oscar Wilde heaven, snuggled into all the artistic bliss of the Left Bank. It was hot. Like sizzling hot. Oppressive. Over 100 degrees with no air movement. And we were so tired. Bone tired. We were coming from Greece, where we had been herded onto a ferry with thousands of people and cars with cages all around us. I just didn't have anything left to give at this tail end of our travels.

We immediately dropped our bags without really noticing our opulent surroundings at L'Hôtel. Tired, hot, thirsty, and hungry, we rounded the corner from our hotel to find a café. Given that it was an off time to eat and the oppressive heat, things were not really busy, and we found a cute café called Le Molière on Rue de Buci. The café was virtually empty. We had a great meal and some chilled beers and wine and just relaxed. Then came time to pay. Our collective exhaustion PLUS the heat wave EQUALED four travelers with their guards down. And just like that, my friend Amy's purse was gone. Stolen. Now we were in a red alert situation. While Amy borrowed a phone to cancel her credit cards, I figured out how to call the police (dial 17, everyone traveling to Paris!!!) We spent the next three hours walking to the police station and filing a report (which I had to assist in translating). And that was my last interaction with Paris. My trust, the city's beauty, my fragile relationship that I had begun to build as a fairly new international traveler----broken---smashed by the crime that exists in any big city that you hope to never see firsthand.

In order to work through my anxiety of seeing Paris again, I decided to psych myself up with everything that I truly love about Paris. I have grown so much and worked through so much of my own personal baggage during this sabbatical. It was time to reconnect with my love of European culture to hype me up for this last stop. I dug up my old love of literature, that had been replaced by 8 years of the self-help genre. I spent hours reading Hemingway, in particular <u>A Moveable Feast</u>, a novel about his time in Paris. I reread my Anaïs Nin books, uncovered my dusty F. Scott Fitzgerald works, and lost myself in the geometric forms of Picasso, hungry to retrace the lives of the famous expats and experience Paris through their literature and art. I listened to Chopin and Edith Piaf and lit my Diptyque Pomander candle. While the scent of cloves and cinnamon filled the air, I perused images of my favorite Hermès patterns and dreamed about owning my own delicate orange silk scarf. I listened to my Tonya Leigh *French Kiss Life* podcasts about her own Parisian inspirations. Instead of being angry about my current American residence in Butler county, I decided to bring all that I love of Paris, France, and Europe in general TO ME.

I researched unique cafés and coffee houses in Pittsburgh and continued on my local "café crawl," where I would spend the day at a café and work on my book and French curriculum. I bought myself Veuve Cliquot champagne and filled one of my Waterford crystal wedding flutes to sip while I ate a slice of homemade fluffy, creamy quiche. I enjoyed pain au chocolat at Mediterra, a European style café in Sewickley, Pennsylvania. I sprayed myself with Chanel Allure and watched French movies. No matter what daily drudgery was going on, like dishes and cleaning drywall dust, I filled my day with as much French mood as possible. On the short flight from Montpellier to Paris, I listened to my Pandora Hôtel Costes station. It's trip hop meets rave. It's everything dark, velvet, purple and leopard print. It's all the things sensual. This was my Paris, and I was determined to see this Paris up close and personal.

Le Marais, Paris

"Breathe Paris in…It nourishes the soul." Victor Hugo

So here Beth and I were, in a gorgeous apartment in the 3rd arrondissement, and I was ready to step into the Paris canvas that I had been creating for the past couple of months. Our apartment was right across the street from Rue St. Paul, the main drag running through the Marais. Our first stop was for lunch. We found a little crêperie where I had a delicious goat cheese, pear, and honey crêpe with a glass of rosé. Coming from Montpellier, where the rosé flowed freely and locally, this petal pink colored heaven had become my new obsession. We then spent the afternoon exploring this busy street-the boulangeries, pâtisseries, épiceries, pharmacie, and the shop with all the roasted chickens set up on the sidewalk. Our apartment host had told us these were the juiciest chickens in all of Paris. We stocked up on Evian at the Franprix and bought a cheap bottle of prosecco at the marchand du vin to toast our Paris experience.

After dropping off our water and prosecco to chill in our apartment, we continued exploring our new neighborhood. We found the Place de Vosges, the oldest square in Paris. Strolling through the center of the Place, I lingered near the Louis XIII statue and took in the 17th century architecture. Walking along the arches that border the square, we stopped to window shop in the numerous art galleries and high-end boutiques. I felt myself breathless-falling in love-with this trendy, yet medieval almost, quartier. Rue des Francs-Bourgeois and Rue Vieille du Temple are a boutique lover's paradise, and Beth and I decided to come back to really shop during our last day here.

Hungry again from all our walking, we headed to Cerise Sur La Pizza, a pizza place I had seen on Instagram. After a homemade margherita pizza with mini bottles of prosecco, we walked back to our apartment. We climbed through those big Parisian French windows to sit and watch the Marais down below with our purchased bottle of prosecco. I fell asleep that night wrapped in all of Paris' magic, feeling connected to all those who had come and gone before me, in search of the art that would both soothe and torment the soul.

The next morning during my shower, I reflected on my fragrance choice for France…*bien sûr*, it had to be Chanel. But not the typical Chanel No. 5. Over the years, I've tried to love Chanel No. 5, because it is so…Parisienne. But I hated it on me, every time. However, last November, I took my family to Paris, and on a whim, I purchased a bottle of Chanel Allure. Although at first taken aback by its heaviness, during the family trip to Paris, I grew to love the somewhat fruity, somewhat vanilla, and somewhat mandarin orangey Allure, and it has become my winter scent. Freshly showered in a cloud of Chanel,

Beth and I started the day in typical French fashion, with a pain au chocolat and a plain croissant. We spent the morning at the Picasso Museum, right near Place des Vosges. There, Beth and I kind of drifted apart, each lost in our own Picasso reverie: Beth, examining the different brush strokes of his works; and me, lost in a fragmented sea of color, deconstructed faces, and rare Antibes inspired landscapes.

Still full from our buttery croissants and not quite ready for lunch, we headed toward Notre Dame. We crossed the Pont (bridge) Notre-Dame, stopping part way across to look at the Seine River and take some pictures. There is something about the view from this bridge that immediately takes me back to reading Ludwig Bemelmans' *Madeline* books. I distinctly remember one Christmas my sister and I receiving Madeline paper dolls-the ones where you had to punch out yourself and fold the little tabs of the clothes over the dolls. Even though my age and the year of that Christmas have faded from my memory, how I felt about Paris when looking at Madeline and the other little girls in 2 straight lines walking toward the Eiffel Tower with Miss Clavel on the cover of that book was EXACTLY how I feel right now: connected to something bigger than myself, curious, inspired.

Notre Dame rose up suddenly to the left as we rounded the corner after crossing the bridge. Last April (2019), a devastating fire in Notre Dame damaged its roof and iconic spire. I had been in Paris in November 2018, just a few months before the fire; I had stood inside this gothic beauty and lit a candle for my aunt who was fighting cancer. As Beth and I quietly stood around the construction barriers, looking at the photos of the fire and restoration that were hanging on the fence, an overwhelming sadness caught me off guard. A sadness for both the loss of part of Paris' history and the loss of my aunt, whose candle I lit just a little over a year ago that still burned in this cathedral.

Right past Notre Dame, we stopped at Shakespeare and Company, the famous bookstore on the Left Bank. This was home of the notorious band of writers, philosophers, and artists whose daily lives centered around understanding the human condition and creating art and literary masterpieces that became the heartbeat of the city. Paris, this Left Bank, provided both the pleasure and the provocation that stimulated these artists. My heart ached a little with the beauty of being able to walk through all the crammed books shelves, both old and new, squeezing through the tiny rooms with the other tourists. I slowly touched the spines of the classics, dreaming of the Hemingway days, overwhelmed by emotion of a time that wasn't even mine. I stood in line and bought my ten euro canvas bag that said Shakespeare and Company on it, luxuriating in the legacy of the 1920's American expats in Paris.

Beth and I continued along the Seine for a bit, passing by the Louvre, heading toward the chic first arrondissement. We stopped off to have lunch at a trendy looking café before Rue St. Honoré. After warming up with a rich French onion soup and a glass of rosé, we decided our dessert was going to be at the Place Vendôme. Since it was

Christmas time, the Ritz hotel, home to the French fashion icon Coco Chanel, had opened a little Christmas chalet right outside the hotel in the elegant Place Vendôme. Here, Beth and I indulged in a 70% Venezuelan signature hot chocolate with a cinnamon apfelstrudel. Snuggled with our chocolat chaud against the December chill, we admired the larger than life Christmas trees beside the Colonne Vendôme. Beth and I window shopped in the world's most luxurious jewelry stores, playfully picking out what we liked and didn't like from jewels that cost more than my whole house. We continued down Rue de la Paix, toward the Opéra Garnier.

At the time of our trip to France, the whole country was affected by a huge strike. The French were protesting President Macron's proposed changes to the pension system, and basically all transportation was shut down. The métro was not running, nor were the busses. Taxis were difficult to get. The Opéra was also closed, as the ballet dancers and other performers were directly affected by this new pension proposal.

As we followed Rue de la Paix to the end, suddenly the Opéra Garnier was in our view. Although we could not go inside because of the strike, I was content to walk around the exterior of this Napoleon III style masterpiece. I don't think I've ever seen a more beautiful building. The green domed roof flanked with Charles Gumery's gilded sculptures of *Harmony* and *Poetry*. The bronze busts of Mozart, Beethoven, etc., found in between the columns on the front. The sheer amount of all that I love and long for in the **Beaux-Arts** on the outside of Palais Garnier could have held my attention for hours.

After a while, we continued a little way and found ourselves at the Galeries Lafayette, one of the most distinguished shopping centers in Paris. It's also pretty famous for its iconic Christmas tree, which changes every year. It's a 65-foot piece of art that hangs from the glass dome in the center of the mall…definitely a sight to see! I had never been to the Galeries Lafayette, and, since we had been out walking for quite some time, we thought we'd pop into the mall to take some pics of the tree and find a restroom. Definitely the most stressful undertaking of our day!! For starters, the mall had five floors, and the bathrooms were located on the very top floor. And it was Christmas time. And this was a famous mall. AND IT WAS SHOPPING IN PARIS. The mall was unbelievably crowded. As Beth and I tried to navigate our way to up to the top floor to find the bathrooms, we were suddenly face to face with the Christmas tree. All 65 feet of it. All reds, pinks, deep blues. Different flower shaped ornaments, twinkle lights, and a fairy angel as the tree topper. The hot, overly crowded designer make-up counters and trendy shops all seem to fade as Beth and I took in the tree. I sent a quick prayer of gratitude to the universe for this unplanned stop at the Galeries Lafayette.

Our Parisian day ended with a long walk back to Le Marais, where we found a small café full of locals and outdoor seating. OUTDOOR SEATING—IN DECEMBER. There, Beth ordered a lovely mojito and I, of course, a glass of rosé. We shared a huge charcuterie tray, and walked home, happily exhausted from our adventures.

Our last morning in Paris, after eating the required buttery deliciousness of two croissants each, we walked the Marais a little slower, stopping to admire boutique windows and actually shop. Late morning, we stopped at the dreamiest café yet, to indulge in one last *chocolat chaud*. The café Carette was situated across from the Place des Vosges. Inside, Beth and I each ordered a chocolat chaud. I have never felt more pampered, more gratitude for travel, more refined, than I did when the waiter brought our hot chocolates. The hot chocolate itself was brought out on a silver tea service. As I tipped the teapot toward my delicate teacup, a stream of pure, melted chocolate bliss filled my cup. Corny or not, Beth and I squealed with delight at our chocolate (I think one of us actually clapped); however, the best was still on its way. Our *serveur* then arrived with our chocolat chaud accompaniment. He brought us a huge silver dish, that matched the teapot, overflowing with the fluffiest, lightest, most luscious cloud of homemade whipped cream I had ever seen. Throughout my travels over the years, I have sought out the best tasting cup of local hot chocolate. This CLEARLY was the winner. Beth and I slowly drank every drop of that hot chocolate and spooned out every mouthful of that whipped cream heaven. I can't really explain what it was, but sitting in that café looking out over the Place des Vosges drinking that chocolate masterpiece, was somehow just as thrilling as the first time I ever laid eyes on all of the famous Parisian landmarks.

Sitting on the runway at Charles de Gaulle airport, getting ready for takeoff for home, I was struck with an emotion for Paris that I can only equate to a lover, and that my previous trips to Paris were also former loves I have had in my past. There was the love that took my virginity in high school and my first trip to Paris; both whom I had been in love with, but still felt vulnerable, unsure, awkward, scared… not sure of what to do. In both instances, I came out on the other side different, aware, and understanding what it means to give yourself away to another, whether it be a person or a city. Then there was the unattached love, and Paris trip, where I was not so afraid, and willing to take on the exciting and adventurous experience that opened the door to my whole self, knowing that it would not last, therefore fearless of making mistakes…an almost reckless encounter. This Paris is one that is alluring and mysterious, sensual and rich, full of all of the self-indulgent things that a true Taurus thrives on. Perhaps the most heartbreaking love, the most heartbreaking Paris, is the one that you have once but know you will never have again. It's seeing the Eiffel Tower for the first time; sitting in a café sipping wine in Saint Germain that first time; walking up the stairs of the Charles de Gaulle-Étoile metro stop and seeing the majestic Arc de Triomphe rise up suddenly in front of you, *THAT FIRST TIME.* You want to bottle up these moments, make them last forever, but you know that's impossible, because there will never be *THIS TIME AGAIN.* So you try to chase it, you try to recreate it, you obsess over it…but it's never to be again. It's the Paris that smells of leather and crisp air, that tastes of cigarettes and red wine. The love that when you think about it, always takes your breath away with the emotional confusion of excitement because it happened, but emptiness because it will NEVER be again. Ohhhhh, there's the inevitable dangerous love, the menacing Paris that I experienced my last trip. I can't resist the draw, I recognize the threat of engaging, but do it anyway. Then finally, for me, for *maintenant* (now), there's the love that is comfortable, wise, sophisticated, and unique. The love, the Paris, that draws you into itself and just KNOWS you and what you want, what you need. The streets that you love to walk over and over because you still find a treasure every time; the love, the Paris, that constantly provides an intellectual challenge, a unending loyalty, even through the unknown (again, another need of all the true Taurus out there).

As my plane lifts off the ground and points upward through the clouds towards the United States, I realize that in giving a voice to my past experiences, AND my trips to Paris, I have a better understanding of myself throughout the accumulated past. It's like all the postcards and memories hitting all at once. That poignancy that defines whatever your life is at that moment. Like every single time I hear "In Your Eyes" by Peter Gabriel, and I'm brought back to that moment of John Cusack holding the boom box overhead, outside of Ione Skye's window, in the movie *Say Anything.* Full and empty at the same time. And guess what? I didn't even see the Eiffel Tower this time.

"And before she could take a full breath of the wonder of how truly far she had come, the wind picked up and a boat sailed by and she reached out." Seth Pitt, artist

We had been holding side angle pose in my hot yoga class for what seemed like an eternity. Sweat dripped down from my fingertips of my extended arm. It was almost time for me to go back to school, my sabbatical was over, so it was time to get back to some normalcy. This was only my second class back in forever to this practice that I adored, so I was struggling physically AND mentally through the poses.

Hot yoga has been a huge part of my life off and on for over ten years. It was like nothing I had ever done before. I hated it at first. It felt uncomfortable, and I had panic attack after panic attack being in a 90 degree room with full on humidity. But for some reason that I've never been able to understand, I KEPT SHOWING UP.

Andrew, my partner in all things life AND work, started going to yoga with me ten years earlier. Within about three months with regular attendance, we became obsessed. The feeling in my body, the connection I felt to myself and the world, was like nothing I had ever felt before. And the breath. There was something magical in maintaining breath with Andrew beside me, flowing through the poses, sweat dripping. It was a high that I never wanted to stop. In those early days, we tried to explain how we felt, what this yoga high was…we would roll out of class, smelling HORRIBLE but not really caring, and go to Aladdin's and eat V-9 vegetable soup and hummus. While sipping hot mint tea, we would try to put our yoga high feelings into words. But we never really could capture what we were feeling. I was 100 percent addicted. Hot yoga carried us through stressful teaching days, Andrew's grandfather's death, and our own personal body struggles. We did partner yoga, 30 day yoga challenges, and spent evenings in his apartment giggling over ayurvedic diet quizzes. We SHOWED UP, on bad days and good days, through snow, rainstorms, and wine headaches.

I don't even remember why now, but I started dropping off in my yoga practice. Over the next years, I would go sporadically. The weight crept on, and my connection to myself dimmed. In an effort to reconnect with the health of my body, I returned to yoga this week. I had been so focused on my physical needs of my overweight body, that I had forgotten the spiritual/mind connection yoga had gifted me before…until holding this side angle pose.

Kelly said, "I can give you all the cues to adjust, fix, and settle in, all of the modifications, all the counts to breathe, but until you connect to the pose and feel it INSIDE YOUR OWN BODY, none of it matters." And just like that, sweat dripping, limbs trembling, I finally understood what it meant "to go within." To stop looking to outside sources for happiness. To stop binging on diversions, whether it be wine, partying, Pringles, chocolate, art, music, language, or busyness. To stop trying to fix myself with journals, courses, psychics, and vision boards. I distractedly finished my practice and hurried home to write THIS. I didn't want to lose THIS:

Travel gifted me an *ESCAPE* from *ESCAPING,* and my return to yoga had softened my defenses to let this lesson in.

I think the little girl me would finally recognize that the universe HAD seen all along all of those wildflowers I picked 45 years ago, and in return, had left a beautifully wrapped gift that I needed in each city I visited. In Florence, I unwrapped courage and passion. In Québec, I opened forgiveness, peace, and love of learning. In Montpellier, culture and global connection were among my gifts. I recognized, too, the angels that were there beside me through my travels...my teachers, Martha from Arkansas, the kind couple from California who shared dinner with me, the girl from the bagel shop who smiled at me every day and knew my order by heart...

A few weeks ago, I found myself at the Appalachian Rock Shop, a rock and crystal emporium hidden away in Western Pennsylvania. What started out as just a fun afternoon out with my daughters, mom, sister, niece, and cousin, became more meaningful by the minute, as I was drawn into the quantum physics of each crystal. Armed with new labradorite, citrine, and selenite for a burst of creativity and insight as I wrapped up my writing, I almost laughed out loud as I realized I was ready to explore the universe again, all past tantrums just that, past. But this time, instead of thinking of 5 year old me struggling to understand the mysteries of what lay beyond, I thought of 90 year old me, raising a glass of champagne and toasting to how proud she was of how much I have grown. *À ta santé.*

I'm beginning to accept the gray in myself. My free spirit trapped in traditional society. Finding beauty and love simultaneously uplifting and oddly melancholy. Connecting constantly with people yet feeling mostly alone. Living a traditional life in Pennsylvania or an exciting cultured European life. I always thought these blacks and whites of mine were all angles and sharp edges, not touching, never blending, always opposites. But now I see, as I finally understood in Picasso's work in Paris, that this geometry really is just all possible viewpoints at once. Or perhaps my blacks and whites are like a Van Gogh, all deliciously swirled together to create the gray. Both make a whole complete work, a whole masterpiece. Armed with this acceptance and the gifts of my travel, I'm ready to SHOW UP for me. And I'll keep showing up, through the discomfort, to the high on the other side.

"Art is not escape, but a way of finding order in chaos, a way of confronting life." Robert Hayden, American poet.

MERCI a million times: To my husband for editing my writing over and over again. To my daughter Juliet for photographing the cover and helping me with format. To my daughter Genevieve for supporting my travels and me being gone from home a lot. To the OFGs for taking me on my first European adventure. *I am so grateful.*

ABOUT THE AUTHOR

Heidi Thomas is a middle school French teacher. When not in the classroom with her beloved Frenchies, she can be found sipping champagne and dreaming about being an expat in the South of France. She lives outside of Pittsburgh, Pennsylvania on an old family farm with her husband Linard, daughters Juliet and Genevieve, and cats Sebastien and Olivier.